Raj Vemuri is one of the most (_ ....
met. However, because of the Lord he is also one of the most tenderhearted
and humble men I have ever known. To know him is to love him.

As an advanced certified licensed clinical pastoral counselor, Raj holds a
national license with the National Christian Counselors Association of
Sarasota, Florida. Additionally, he serves as an international representative
of the Sarasota Academy of Christian Counselors. He is not only certified
in the use of the Arno Profile System but he also teaches individuals who
want to become A.P.S. Certified. He is established as a well-respected
counselor and educator.

—Richard G. Arno, PhD
Author and Founder: National Christian Counselors Association
Sarasota, Florida

Raj is ordained and is a clergy member of the National Conservative
Christian Church since early 2006. I know him to be a man of integrity
with a loving family. Raj holds a number of degrees, including two
doctorates in counseling and psychology. He is a classroom teacher at the
college level and has earned the respect of many academic colleagues.

Raj is effective in Christian ministry and is accountable to this organization and our presbytery. He reports to our board regularly. We admire
him for the reputation he has earned and are happy to call him a member
in good standing with a Certificate of Ordained Minister of Pastoral
Counseling. Rev. Raj Vemuri is a man of sincerity and integrity. He has
great insights into truth, and I recommend his book to you. I hold him
in high regard.

—Rev. Dr. Donald Struble
President, National Conservative Christian Church
Sarasota, Florida

Raj is a board member of the Morning Star Counseling Center in Portage,
Michigan. I first came to know Raj when he joined my ministry team
of Christian volunteers at the Kalamazoo County Jail in Kalamazoo,
Michigan, where I was serving as the chaplain. He, being a convert from
Hinduism and from India, was an unusual and unique individual on our
jailhouse ministry team.

Raj soon impressed me with one major theme. He was a seeker of the truth. Of course, that is at the very core of sanctification, the goal of biblical counseling. I believe that you will be challenged by Raj's exploration of his topic and you, no doubt, will be encouraged to seek out the truth and then be motivated to implement it.

—Tom Dymond
Executive Director, Morning Star Counseling Center
Portage, Michigan

Raj is a man of rare intellectual capacity. Yet he is a man of great spiritual sensitivity as well. This former Hindu Brahmin knows what it is like to forsake all and follow Christ. May this book be a catalyst for change in your life and may you always walk closer with the Master as Raj outlines in this uncompromising book.

The life of Christ is so evident in Raj's life. May this abundant life invade your life as you read this powerful book. This is a time for unconventional men and women with an unconventional message. Raj is just such a man.

Rev. Charles Robinson
Pastor, Tree of Life International Prayer & Praise Center
Austin, Texas

FROM HINDUISM TO CHRIST

FROM
HINDUISM
TO
CHRIST

A FORMER HINDU BRAHMIN LOOKS AT WORLD RELIGIONS
AND THE POWERFUL TRUTHS OF THE CHRISTIAN FAITH

RAJ VEMURI, PH.D.

Pleasant Word (a division of WinePress Publishing, PO Box 428, Enumclaw, WA 98022) functions only as book publisher. As such, the ultimate design, content, editorial accuracy, and views expressed or implied in this work are those of the author.

Unless otherwise noted, all Scriptures are taken from the *Holy Bible, New International Version®, NIV®*. Copyright © 1973, 1978, 1984 by Biblica, Inc.™ Used by permission of Zondervan. All rights reserved worldwide.

Scripture references marked KJV are taken from the *King James Version* of the Bible.

Scripture references marked NASB are taken from the *New American Standard Bible*, © 1960, 1963, 1968, 1971, 1972, 1973, 1975, 1977 by The Lockman Foundation. Used by permission.

ISBN 13: 978-1-4141-1493-4
ISBN 10: 1-4141-1493-1
Library of Congress Catalog Card Number: 2009905258

This book is affectionately dedicated to the three most beautiful and precious women in my life:

My mother, Seeta,
who has shown so much unconditional love,
compassion, tolerance, patience, and understanding.
She is a real blessing from the Lord.

My wife, Vicki,
a woman who loves the Lord and is very loving,
patient, and has been kind enough to stick with me through
thick and thin and is always supportive and is,
undoubtedly, my better half.

My daughter, Danielle,
who always has so much love to give and
maintains a sweet and gentle spirit. She
knows how to make my day in a moment.
To me, she is an angel sent from heaven.

CONTENTS

A Special Note xiii

Some Key Scriptures xv

Acknowledgments xvii

Preface xix

Section One: A Personal Journey

  1. A Brief History of India 1

  2. My Family Background 5

  3. Growing Up a Hindu Brahmin 13

  4. My Religious Upbringing 17

  5. Emotional Struggles 23

  6. Coming to the United States 31

  7. Seeking and Searching the Truth 35

  8. Why Learn About Other Faiths? 39

  Conclusion and Final Note 45

Section Two: Hinduism: That Old Time Religion

  9. Who is a Hindu? 49

10. The Belief System 53

11. Salvation 63

12. Hindu Sacred Texts 71

13. Three Main Gods. 79

14. The Consorts. 85

15. Other Important Gods. 89

16. The Caste System—The Four Varnas 93

Section Three: Customs, Practices, Rituals, and Worship

17. Customs and Rituals. 101

18. Worship and Practices. 105

19. Hinduism Versus Christianity. 109

Section Four: Christianity

20. Facts about the Christian Faith. 125

21. The Trinity—God in Three Persons 131

22. The Bible—The Word of God 145

23. The Church 153

Section Five: Other Major World Religions

24. The Teachings of Buddhism 169

25. Central Beliefs of Buddhism 173

26. Christianity Compared with Buddhism 181

27. The Teachings and Central Beliefs of Islam 187

28. Christianity Compared with Islam 199

Section Six: Christian Apologetics

29. Defending the Faith 219

30. What Is God Like? 231

Section Seven: The Conclusion

31. My Personal Testimony 243

Bibliography 251
Reference to the Hindu Scriptures 257
Reference to the Holy Bible 259
Reference to the Holy Qur'an 263
About the Author 265

A SPECIAL NOTE

THE MOTIVATION FOR writing this book stemmed from a strong desire to present the truth based strictly on my perspective, convictions, understanding of the Word of God, and my life experiences. For example, discussions on such topics as the sin nature and conviction are written in terms of my experiences concerning the awesome forgiveness and freedom that the Lord has given me. Thus its contents are not meant to judge, target, or stereotype any individual(s) in terms of their particular faith or belief system. Nevertheless, recognizing that some may find it to be offensive, I offer my sincere apologies to those individual(s).

This book is mainly targeted towards those who identify themselves as "saved" or "born-again believers" that is, those who have accepted Jesus Christ as their personal Lord and Savior. Thus, hopefully, the book will serve to educate Christian believers about other major world religions in order that they too might know how to approach skeptics and be better prepared to effectively share the gospel with all whom they might meet. While reading this book, I highly advise each individual to keep an open mind.

My sincere hope, desire, and prayer are that individuals who read this book will find it informative, educational, and helpful from a spiritual standpoint. More importantly, I hope that it will offer encouragement and be thought provoking in terms of any questions that nonbelievers might have about God, Jesus, heaven, hell, salvation, and eternity. Moreover, it is my sincere desire that this book will inspire readers to search for the truth as it relates to God, especially in terms of one's own personal faith journey and salvation.

SOME KEY SCRIPTURES

I WOULD LIKE to share some key Scriptures that touched my heart as I was writing this book.

"My people are destroyed for lack of knowledge."

—Hos. 4:6, NKJV

"...I have become all things to all men, that I might by all means save some."

—1 Cor. 9 22, NKJV

"Be diligent to present yourself approved to God, a worker who does not need to be ashamed, rightly dividing the word of truth."

—2 Tim. 2:15, NKJV

"...always be ready to give a defense to everyone who asks you a reason for the hope that is in you."

—1 Peter 3:15, NKJV

"All Scripture is given by inspiration of God, and is profitable for doctrine, for reproof, for correction, for instruction in righteousness."

—2 Tim. 3:16, NKJV

"But our God is in heaven; He does whatever He pleases. Their idols are silver and gold, the work of men's hands. They have mouths, but they do not speak; Eyes they have, but they do not see; They have ears, but they do not hear; Noses they have, but they do not smell; they have hands, but they do not handle; Feet they have, but they do not walk; Nor do they mutter through their throat. Those who make them are like them; so is everyone who trusts in them."

—Ps. 115:3–8, NKJV

"Jesus said to him, 'I am the way, the truth, and the life. No man comes to the Father except through Me.'"

—John 14:6, NKJV

"For God so loved the world that He gave His only begotten Son, that whoever believes in Him should not perish but have everlasting life."

—John 3:16, NKJV

"Jesus answered and said to him, 'Most assuredly, I say to you, unless one is born again, he cannot see the kingdom of God.'"

—John 3:3, NKJV

"Do not marvel that I said to you, 'You must be born again.'"

—John 3:7, NKJV

"That if you confess with your mouth the Lord Jesus and believe in your heart that God has raised Him from the dead, you will be saved. For with the heart one believes to righteousness, and with the mouth confession is made to salvation."

—Rom. 10:9–10, NKJV

"For whoever calls upon the name of the Lord shall be saved."

—Rom. 10:13, NKJV

"Nor is there salvation in any other, for there is no other name under heaven given among men by which we must be saved."

—Acts 4:12, NKJV

"For it is written: 'As I live, says the Lord, Every knee shall bow to Me, And every tongue shall confess to God.'"

—Rom. 14:11, NKJV

ACKNOWLEDGMENTS

MANY PEOPLE HAVE played a key role in the birth of this book, and I gratefully acknowledge those who have contributed significantly to it.

My loving wife, Vicki, has worked very diligently reading and editing the manuscript to help produce a finished product. I am very blessed to have a godly woman as my best friend and life partner.

All my brothers and sisters who have stood by me proving time and time again that "blood is thicker than water."

Dr. Richard Arno, author, founder and president of National Christian Counselors Association, Sarasota, Florida. Dr. Arno was my clinical supervisor during my doctoral program at NCCA.

Dr. Donald Struble, president of National Conservative Christian Church, Sarasota, Florida. Dr. Struble ordained me through NCCC, a governing body that oversees my spiritual accountability.

Mr. Tom Dymond, executive director, Morning Star Counseling Center, Portage, Michigan. Tom has been my spiritual mentor and advisor for the past nine years and has counseled and advised me on many important issues of life from a biblical standpoint.

My good friend, Cliff, who always encouraged me with his positive outlook on life and the time he spent exchanging many real-life principles in light of biblical standards. We both share an interest in the study of apologetics.

Dirk, my good friend whom I met at a local bookstore. He has always challenged me to come up with some thought-provoking answers from the Word of God concerning delicate and difficult issues of life. I feel quite challenged each time I speak with him. God has used him to sharpen my knowledge concerning the Word of God.

Last, but not least, my good friend and psychology adjunct instructor colleague, Dr. Richard Marsella. He is a very wise, intelligent, and down-to-earth individual who has challenged me both cognitively as well as spiritually on many occasions. I am thankful for his knowledge, experience, education, training, and wisdom.

PREFACE

THROUGHOUT THIS BOOK, especially as I share my life grow-ing up as a Hindu Brahmin, I use many personal and spiritual terms. However, Section Two is strictly dedicated to a discussion of Hinduism. This section also explains many details on the Hindu religion such as its beliefs, rituals, gods, goddesses, the caste system, and other significant topics. This section not only serves to assist the reader in understanding and relating to the Hindu religion, but also sets the stage for providing a better understanding of where I am coming from and where I stand in regards to this religion.

This book also presents a chapter on Christianity, which discusses aspects concerning the Word of God (the Bible) in great detail, as well as a separate chapter on Buddhism and Islam, in which the beliefs and teachings of these religious systems are com-pared to that of the Christian faith. And, finally, special attention is given to Christian apologetics. This section is very important since it provides insight into the beliefs and practices of Christianity and provides reasons for why I believe that Christianity is the only true religion.

The chapters on Hinduism were written for non-Hindus, especially for Christians. Most Hindus already possess a great deal of knowledge concerning the beliefs and teachings of their religion.

Similarly, the chapters on Christianity were written for anyone who lacks an in-depth understanding regarding God, Jesus, the Holy Spirit, sin, salvation, and the Bible.

As for the section on Christian apologetics, I strongly recommend that readers approach this chapter with an open mind. Furthermore, readers should also pay close attention to the details discussed, as this section defends the Word of God as truth and provides substantial evidence to support the claims that Jesus made about Himself being the Lord, the one and only God and the Messiah.

While seeking and searching for truth as it relates to God and His character, I studied many major world religions, in particular their beliefs and teachings. As I conducted an in-depth study of these various religions, I became increasingly curious, which further led me to specifically focus on the study of apologetics. An apologist isn't a person who is apologizing for something all the time but rather is someone who defends the faith.

The study of Christian apologetics further motivated me to search for and find the truth, both from a theoretical and an academic standpoint. I believe that during this time of searching, God, who knew my heart's desire, was already preparing the path that He wanted me to take for the rest of my life. My part in this matter only involved keeping an open mind. But once the truth was revealed to me, I also had to be obedient to God's direction.

SECTION ONE

A PERSONAL JOURNEY

CHAPTER 1

A BRIEF HISTORY
OF INDIA

INDIA, THE COUNTRY of my birth, is one of the few nations whose history notably rises to the level of being one of the grand epics in terms of world history. I recall that Mr. Jawaharlal Nehru, India's first prime minister, once described India as a bundle of contradictions held together by strong but invisible threads.

India's history dates back at least 5,000 years, although some still differ regarding the exact date. For example, some argue that India's history dates back to approximately 3200 B.C. when Hinduism was first founded. The country of India, named after the river Indus, is home to one of the world's oldest and richest civilizations. In the book *A Traveler's History of India*, Mr. Tammita-Delgoda notes that "India's history stretches back for more than 4,000 years and, alongside Egypt and Mesopotamia, it is one of the very cradles of civilization—the origin of many of the ideas, philosophies, and movements which have shaped the destiny of mankind."

India is located in the southeast part of the continent of Asia and is bordered on its western side by China, Nepal, and Pakistan. The Himalayan mountain chain lies along its northern border. India's coastal borders are formed by the Bay of Bengal in the east, the Arabian Sea in the west, and the Indian Ocean in the south.

The Europeans, including the British, Dutch, French, and Portuguese, had a notable influence on Indian culture during periods of rule by these countries, as well as by the Persians, currently known as the Iranians. Notably, it was a Persian ruler who built the Taj Mahal, which to date is still considered the eighth wonder of the world and the most symmetrical building on the planet. Indian culture was also influenced during periods of invasion by the Afghans and Arabians, as well as by westerners. India is a country that encourages diversity in terms of its acceptance of different religious beliefs, use of languages (and dialects), and cultural makeup. It is this great diversity that attracts many to study India, making it a fascinating place to visit.

The Indian population is accepting or tolerant of many religions, but the two main religions practiced in India are Hinduism and Islam. Of these, Hinduism is the predominant religion, which is practiced by approximately 80 percent of the Indian population. Roughly 10 percent of the Indian population is Muslim and, thus, practice Islam. Other religions practiced in India include those that are less popular, such as Buddhism, Christianity, Jainism, Sikhism, Bahai and Judaism. There are also agnostics, atheists, humanistic secularists, and those who practice New Age spirituality.

Hinduism supports a belief in the caste system, which is a system based on old traditions. According to Hinduism, there are four different castes, namely, Brahmins, Kshatriyas, Vysyas, and Shudras. Of these, the Brahmin caste is considered to be the highest caste. Members of this caste traditionally belong to the priestly background.

There are seventeen major languages spoken in India and more than 800 dialects, but Hindi is the official national language. Approximately 30 percent of the Indian population has adopted Hindi as their primary tongue. English is unofficially considered the second national language because of its importance in commercial, national, and political communication purposes. The other official languages include Assamese, Bengali, Gujarati, Kannada, Kashmiri, Malayalam, Marathi, Oriya, Punjabi, Sanskrit, Sindhi, Tamil, Telugu, and Urdu. The 17th spoken language is unofficially known as Hindustani, a language that consists of a mix of Hindi and Urdu and is widely spoken throughout the northern regions of India.

India gained its independence from the British on August 15, 1947. It adopted a federal republic as its form of government. India is currently the largest democracy in the world.

India consists of twenty-eight States and seven Union Territories. Its capital is New Delhi. The country's most populated cities include Mumbai (formerly known as Bombay), Kolkata (formerly known as Calcutta), and New Delhi. Approximately 16.4 million people live in Mumbai, approximately 13.2 million live in Kolkata, and approximately 12.8 million live in New Delhi. Other major cities include Chennai (formerly known as Madras) with a population of approximately 6.4 million, Bangalore with approximately 5.7 million people, Hyderabad with approximately 5.5 million people, Ahmedabad with a population of approximately 5 million, and Pune with approximately 4 million people.

The population of India is approximately 1.13 billion, ranking India as the second most populated place in the world, right behind China. In terms of its geographical size, India ranks seventh place in the world. Although India's total geographical area encompasses only approximately one-third that of the United States, its population exceeds the United States by three times.

Despite India having made great strides in the areas of medicine, technology, and infrastructure, its economy is still based largely on its agricultural output. India also has a large iron and steel industry. It currently produces many different types of manufactured goods.

The climate of India fluctuates based on seasonality but is best known for being tropical monsoon-like in the south and temperate in the north.

The official currency of India is the rupee. Several other countries such as Mauritius, Nepal, Pakistan, and Sri Lanka also use this currency. The origin of the word rupee can be traced back to Sanskrit; it means *silver*. The term used to refer to a coin is paisa for one and paise for multiple coins. Thus, one rupee equals 100 paise.

Traveling by train is the most efficient means to sightsee throughout India. The country has one of the world's oldest railway systems as well as one of the largest in terms of the area it services. India also has six international airports, one each in Bangalore, Chennai, New Delhi, Hyderabad, Kolkata, and Mumbai. Western influence is becoming increasingly influential in many areas of India, especially in medicine, technology, media, and the film industry. India produces approximately 1,400 films a year, which makes it the top film-producing country in the world.

CHAPTER 2

MY FAMILY
BACKGROUND

I AM THE youngest of eight children (four girls and four boys) born into a Hindu Brahmin family. I was very blessed to have been born into a family where there was so much love, affection, understanding, support, compassion, and tolerance. In my family, there was always plenty of unconditional love to spread around.

My parents were the type of people who would best fit the description of being "one in a million." My father was a self-made man who was a very practical, down-to-earth, hard-working, diligent, wise, and honest gentleman. By nature he was very transparent in that he did not hide any of his faults. He did not believe in playing games and he also did not believe in beating around the bush. For the better part of his life he was a schoolteacher.

Later on, my father assumed the position of headmaster or principal of a high school in Hyderabad, and he eventually became principal of a junior college from which he later retired. He maintained high morals and reared his children to maintain the utmost integrity. My earliest recollections were that he was not only very hard working but also was one of the wisest persons that I have ever known. Raising eight children on a schoolteacher's salary was not an easy task.

Out of necessity, my father learned to use the family's finances wisely. Yet he made many sacrifices along the way. He was a devoted husband and wise father. In general, he acted in a positive, productive manner and was an effective role model both at home and at school. As the high priest of our family, he made sure that all of his children were reared to understand details concerning such things as the caste system, as well as the gods and goddesses. Sadly, my father died of cancer in February 1996.

My mother gave unconditional love to all of her children. She had many noble qualities. One such quality that she consistently demonstrated was her ability to refrain from speaking negatively about others behind their backs, no matter what they had done or regardless of how they were treating others.

At birth, I was diagnosed with Indian Childhood Cirrhosis and had to stay in the hospital for an extended period. Although many family members took turns keeping an eye on me while I was in the hospital, it was my mother who spent most nights sleeping on the floor to make sure that I was being properly cared for. I am very thankful and blessed to have had such a loving and devoted woman as my mother. Sadly, she also died of cancer, in September 2004. As long as I live, I will have a special place in my heart for both of my parents, but in particular for my mother since we shared an especially close bond due to the fact that I was her youngest child.

My family is considered to be well educated and knowledgeable. At the very least, all of my seven siblings have an undergraduate degree. This also holds true for all my brothers-and sisters-in-law.

My eldest sister, Nirmala, studied law even though she never practiced in this field. She currently resides in India and recently retired after working thirty-six years as a senior branch manager of a bank in Hyderabad. Before retirement, she handled three branches as branch manager and chief manager.

In many ways Nirmala takes after my father; she is practical, down-to-earth, and lives a structured way of life. She lived next door to my parents and had daily contact with them while providing continued assistance towards their care. It was through this daily contact that I believe she accumulated much wisdom over a period of many years.

Nirmala is a giving person and maintains a humble heart. She is ready and willing to serve and contribute to others in any way that she can. She is a woman of few words, but each time she speaks she shares her wisdom and experience.

My eldest brother, Radha, currently resides in Michigan. He is a well-known and highly-respected oncologist and hematologist and a successful physician. He has done much for me. He sponsored me for a green card that allowed me to pursue a higher education in the United States and he assumed all of my financial and immigration responsibilities during my early years as a student.

Radha was valedictorian of his graduating class of 1970 from the Institute of Medical Sciences in Hyderabad, India. He was a recipient of two gold medals in his field of medicine. He came to the United States in 1971 for further training and ended up living in Detroit, where he completed his residency and internship in internal medicine at Henry Ford Hospital as well as at Mt. Sinai hospital. In 1976, he moved to Kalamazoo, Michigan, with his wife, Karen.

In 1995, Radha was appointed clinical professor at the College of Human Medicine at Michigan State University. Since 1994, and up until recently, he served as medical director for West Michigan Cancer Center, P.C. My brother is a sports-oriented person and has won numerous awards and trophies in shuttle badminton, tennis, etc. In addition, he also plays excellent table tennis and is very good at golf, which happens to be his favorite hobby or interest.

I consider my brother to be a very successful physician, a devoted husband, a caring and loving father, an understanding and loving brother. He has some very special qualities that contribute to his innate ability to exercise a great bedside manner. He is forgiving, compassionate, and lives a well-balanced life.

My second-oldest brother, Sudhakar, currently resides in India. He recently retired after working 25 years as a public relations officer in a bank in Hyderabad. Although he had many opportunities to come to the United States, he chose to stay in India and assumed the major part of caregiving for my parents.

My brother is extremely sports-oriented. Sports to him are second nature. During his college years, he was a champion in boxing, cycling, pole vault, shot put, and many other team games. He worked for Food Corporation of India for about eleven-and-a-half years. He then started working for a bank and remained there for about twenty-four years.

While working for a bank, Sudhakar held several positions such as assistant manager, manager, special officer, and public relations officer. In 1991, he became an international certified umpire in shuttle badminton. He officiated in three Olympics consecutively: Barcelona, Spain (1992); Atlanta, Georgia (1996); and Sydney, Australia (2000).

He also officiated at three World Championships, three Thomas and Uber Cup Preliminaries, two Thomas and Uber Cup Finals, three Grand Prix Finals, two Asian Games, two World Cup Finals, and many other international tournaments held in India and abroad. Sudhakar retired as an umpire in 2004 at the Singapore Open and has been an Asian referee ever since. He has refereed tournaments (as a chief referee) in India, Iran, Malaysia, Pakistan, and Sri Lanka. From time to time he also conducts training courses and workshops for umpires in different countries in Asia.

My brother is an all-around pleasant and enjoyable person, a charismatic and charming individual, and he has a great sense of humor. He has a magnetic type of personality, meaning people cling to him because they enjoy his company.

My second-eldest sister, Swarna, currently resides in Oklahoma. She earned three bachelor degrees: a bachelor of science (B.S.) with triple major in chemistry, math, and physics; a bachelor of education (B.Ed) in English and math; and a bachelor of science (B.S.) in special education, specializing in learning disabilities and mental retardation. In addition, she also earned a graduate degree (M.S.) in school psychology. She has earned several certifications in areas such as early childhood education, psychometric assessment, and others. When she lived in the country of Libya, Swarna ran home schools for all the Asian children from 1982 till 1989.

Swarna worked as a math and science teacher at Bharatiya Vidya Bhavan, India, from 1990 until 1995. From 1998 until 2003, she worked as a special education teacher in the Tulsa, Oklahoma, public schools. Since 2003, she has been working as a school psychologist responsible for counseling, evaluation, resources, etc.

During the early years of my childhood, Swarna was the one who oversaw my care more than any of my other siblings. My sister is a good cook, especially of Indian dishes. She has a pleasant personality. She is very good at what she does and she is always willing and ready to reach out to others if and when the need arises. She maintains a simple lifestyle and does not beat around the bush. With her, what you see is what you get. She and I are both in the same field of counseling and psychology.

My third-eldest brother, Ramesh, resides in Maryland. He is very close to being a jack-of-all-trades as well as master of them all too. In one sense, he is like a modern-day Albert Einstein, at least in my opinion. He is knowledgeable in many areas of life and hence possesses extensive knowledge about movies, politics, sports, humor, education, literature, science, and health.

Ramesh earned a bachelor's degree (B.S.) majoring in biology and earned two graduate degrees: a master of science (M.S.) in cell physiology and a master of philosophy in biochemistry. He also has an earned doctorate (Ph.D.) in biochemistry. He studied at Hadassah Medical School, Hebrew University, Israel, as well as at Erasmus University, Rotterdam, the Netherlands.

Ramesh has received numerous honors and awards in his field and has published extensively in various scientific journals. He has had several prestigious career positions and titles from that of being a research scientist, director, and health science administrator. Currently, he is working for the National Institute of Health as a scientist and also as a chief of the Scientific Review Office.

My brother lives the life of a scholar and yet tries to be very simple and humble. He does not give others the impression or idea that he knows a lot. In other words, he can converse with ease with anyone at any level. He has a great sense of humor and knows how to make people laugh. He too is a sports-oriented person, with some achievements in shuttle badminton, and he also plays table tennis.

My third-eldest sister, Lakshmi, resides in Virginia with her husband. She has a bachelor's degree (B.S.) in accounting. She worked for a bank for about six years before moving to the United States. She has taken several courses in information systems and switched careers working on and off in the software industry before starting her own software consultancy business.

Currently, Lakshmi is the chief executive officer (her husband is the president) of a small computer software consultancy firm. My sister has a great sense of humor and it does not take much to make her laugh. She is sensitive to other people's needs and makes herself available to meet those needs when they come to her attention. She is also a good cook. She is good at managing her time and finances and often presents herself to be a good role model both at home and to those outside.

My fourth-eldest sister, Padma, resides in Chennai, India. She earned a bachelor's degree (bachelors in commerce). Right after graduation, she started her career working at the prestigious Indian Overseas Bank in 1983. She has put in about 26 years of service with the bank.

Padma is also a good cook. She has a great sense of humor. She loves to make others happy and at peace. She is kind hearted and with any encouragement she gives, she is very honest. She is hard working both at home as well as at the bank. She is a good wife and a good mother.

I am the youngest of my seven siblings. I currently reside in Florida, along with my wife and daughter. During my early years, I failed the 7th, 10th, and 12th grades of my schooling. Thus I was considered to be the brown sheep of my family. Later on in life, I went on to earn three doctoral degrees. Some folks have asked me why I needed all of these degrees. It is because of the people I love.

I am blessed to have a godly wife whom I most definitely consider to be my better half. I dedicated my first doctoral dissertation in her honor. The second was earned in honor of my parents, and the last one was earned in honor of my daughter, who has Down Syndrome. I attended a Hindu school from kindergarten through grade four and a Christian school from Grades five through seven. As I recall, the Christian school that I attended practiced a daily ritual whereby all students were instructed to sing a song about Jesus each morning after their arrival. The song that we were supposed to sing was written in Telugu, my mother tongue. This song translated into English goes something like this, "Jesus Christ is very much alive today and He lives in my heart."

All three of my older brothers also attended this Christian school, but I don't recall if any of them sang this song. As we were all born into the Hindu Brahmin caste, we were not obligated or encouraged to take part in this ritual. Thus, most likely they either did not sing along with the other students or they just mouthed the words. As for me, I chose to sing the song even though I had some mixed feelings as I was doing it. In actuality, I enjoyed singing the song despite being of the Hindu religion. I decided not to let anyone in my family know about my participation in this ritual, especially my parents. Author William Cowper once said, "God works in mysterious ways." I can personally relate to this statement since God indeed was working mysteriously behind the scenes to prepare me for the plan He had for my life.

From grades eight through ten (high school), I attended a school that was predominately populated by Muslims and had a Muslim headmaster (principal). In my early years, I was exposed to various faiths and beliefs by way of contact with other students and friends who had a religious affiliations differing from mine. In this way, I gained a great deal of knowledge about other beliefs and faiths. This increased my knowledge about what other religions taught and spurred my curiosity as to which one if any was based solely on truth.

Even after coming to the United States in the fall of 1982, I had many friends who belonged to other religions and they, too, shared their beliefs and faith with me. Through association alone, I received in-depth knowledge on various religions, which in turn motivated me to find out just who God is and what He is like and to seek out and search for truth.

CHAPTER 3

GROWING UP
A HINDU BRAHMIN

W HO IS A Brahmin (sometimes also known as Brahman) and why is it such a big deal to be one? In order to understand or define a Brahmin, it is important to describe one, but this is not easy to do in just a few words or lines. In order to understand who a Brahmin is, an individual needs to study certain sacred texts.

In her book *Hinduism: An Illustrative Introduction*, well-known and respected author, Ganga Somany, provides a detailed description of a Brahmin. "In the Rig Veda Samhita the term Brahman is used in the sense of sacred knowledge or sacred speech, a hymn or incantation. Vac, the holy utterance, is personified as Brahman. Thus, by Brahman is meant mantra or prayer. In the Brahmanas, the Brahman is identified with the ritual or sacrifice. In the Aranyakas and Upanishads, however, Brahman is considered as the ultimate source and essence of the universe."

Brahman is derived from the root "brh," meaning to swell or permeate. Ms. Somany further adds, "It [Brahman] is the supreme being, regarded as impersonal and divested of all quality and action." When Maya (which is an illusion) is compared with a Brahmin, the difference is obvious because Maya is perceived as a relative reality where as the Brahmin is perceived as an absolute reality.

Being born into a Brahmin family has its privileges. But it also has its challenges and limitations. When an individual identifies with and is living as a Brahmin, he must live up to certain rules and expectations. For example, he must participate in daily early morning prayers, visit temples, practice various home rituals such as pujas, engage in celebrations, recite prayers, and pray to gods and goddesses. Traditionally, Brahmins are considered to be of the highest caste. But with the passage of time, changes have come about not only in terms of how individuals view these traditions but also in terms of how strictly they hold fast to maintaining them.

For example, there was a time when Brahmins were mostly involved in engaging and performing various spiritual and godly activities. But in recent times, the acceptance by the Indian culture for Brahmins to enter the field of medicine, technology, film industry, education, politics, and business has been growing. Non-Brahmins still look to Brahmins for spiritual guidance and wisdom in dealing with matters concerning almost all areas of life.

A true Brahmin is known to possess many qualities and characteristics that are similar to but definitely not equal to that of God. The word Brahmin or Brahman is derived from Brahma, who is part of the trinity or trimurthi. Although it may seem strange to some, many Indians are very good at guessing the caste of their fellow Indians. In other words, they seem to be able to easily identify which Indians are Brahmins from among a room full of strangers.

This ease is attributed to a difference in how Brahmins present themselves in public, both in outward appearance as well as in terms of their cognitive abilities. The way an individual walks and talks and also how he chooses to dress or how he thinks, and the very nature of an individual's personality speaks volumes. It is not always easy to detect and identify a Brahmin but it is not wholly impossible either.

Traveling abroad is one of the best ways to get a hands-on education about other nationalities as well as to broaden an individual's perspectives on how others of differing faiths view life. Often it also heightens an individual's appreciation for the things that they have been blessed with. For example, here in the United

States we have the right to vote and the right to choose our religion and beliefs. A few years back, I took one of my American friends on a trip to India for sightseeing and to personally experience my culture. We were on our way to visit a very old Hindu temple when we were confronted by a teenage male who, for no apparent reason, wanted to pick a fight with my friend. According to my culture, guests are the responsibility of the Indian family in which they are being accompanied while traveling or while staying in my homeland. Thus I had to intervene on my friend's behalf to try to bring the situation to resolution peaceably. As I was getting ready to speak to this young man, his uncle interrupted him and told him to leave both of us alone. There is an age-old sentiment that one should not intentionally or voluntarily harm or insult a Brahmin. And, apparently, this young man's uncle had identified me as a Brahmin.

My grandfather once told me that when a Brahmin gets hurt or is insulted, the gods will be angry and they will not be content until they get retribution. This kind of thinking is in keeping with that of Isaac Newton's third law of gravity that for every action there is an equivalent and opposite reaction. Similarly, Paul related in the Bible, "Do not be deceived, God is not mocked; for whatever a man sows, that he will also reap" (Gal. 6:7, NKJV). Thus if individuals perform harmful acts they will reap the same type of consequences.

In the same way, the Bible also teaches that each time we sin, God forgives us the very moment we repent and ask for forgiveness. But since God is just, He will in some way need to address that sin. In other words, each thought, each action, each choice, and each deed will have a consequence whether individuals like it or not.

The life of a Brahmin is not always easy because of associated rules and very high expectations of self and others. A Brahmin is expected to obey and follow all associated rules as well as live up to these high expectations. What are these rules or expectations and who makes them? Some can be found in the sacred texts and others can be made or added as time passes. Some rules or expectations may include, but are not limited to, maintaining pure thoughts, engaging in daily spiritual activities, meditation, and performing pujas and prayers.

If a Brahmin fails to do this, he not only risks losing self-respect but also the respect of others. If the individual trying to apply these concepts fails, others may become disappointed. The shortcomings involved with applying these concepts is that an individual should never put any human on a pedestal nor should one expect another to live up to excessively high expectations.

In the Bible we read, "To whom much has been committed, of him they will ask the more" (Luke 12:48, NKJV). When Brahmins apply this Scripture to their lives, they are expected to live a life that is almost perfect since a Brahmin is put on a pedestal. Although some Brahmins may disagree, an individual may never be equal to God. But at least on a human level, an individual can always try to outdo other humans. From a spiritual standpoint, Brahmins are expected to outdo the other three castes. All of these expectations, rules, and rituals have the potential to put much pressure on an individual's life. Not living up to these expectations may lead to a great deal of stress. Of course, every individual has to learn to deal with certain drawbacks, weaknesses, and limitations.

CHAPTER 4

MY RELIGIOUS
UPBRINGING

GROWING UP AS a Brahmin, I was required to practice certain traditions such as participating in religious ceremonies, visiting temples on a regular basis, and attending religious plays. Many, if not most, Hindus pray to more than one god and possibly more than one goddess. I was no exception to this practice; while a Hindu, I favored some gods above others.

I was completely willing to surrender all of my thoughts, desires, actions, plans, decisions, and deeds to these gods. But I was motivated by fear, as well as out of a sense of obligation. Since I am the youngest child in my family, I did not have the freedom or liberty to speak out against these family traditions, much less speak out or give my opinions regarding any of the Hindu gods or goddesses.

My favorite god was Hanuman, also known as the monkey god. Lord Hanuman has a face and tail that resembles a monkey. But from the neck down, he has a human body that looks to be very strong and muscular. In addition to the Hanuman god, I also looked up and admired and prayed to Lord Krishna, who happens to be the eighth avatar or incarnation of Lord Vishnu. Many Hindu texts quote Lord Krishna as being one of the most favorite avatars of Vishnu. There were two other gods that I prayed to on a fairly consistent basis. One of them was Lord Ganesha the other was Lord Venkateswara.

I had a happy, contented childhood up until I reached twelve or thirteen years of age. After that is when all of my troubles began. First, I chose friends in the neighborhood who were known as troublemakers. Based on the viewpoint of a Brahmin, I became involved in a lot of things that were considered to be wrong. For example, I was lying to those around me, stealing, showing disrespect to my parents and siblings and basically acting out my rebellious inclinations. In addition, I was verbally abusing those around me, picking arguments with anyone I could find who would entertain my goings on, and I had very unhealthy eating habits.

Furthermore, I had a great deal of pent-up anger. At a moment's notice I was quick to lash out at anyone around me for only minor disagreements. My family would leave me alone when I got angry; they thought that I might do something worse that they might regret later for provoking me to anger. I recall one incident whereby I was with some of my trouble-making friends who were taking bets as to which one of the gang might be the bravest to do something wrong. After I challenged them to think that I was the bravest, they put me to the test and suggested that I steal a motor scooter. The plan was for me to drive it around for just a couple of minutes and then return it to its original location in the parking lot near a busy intersection. I accepted the challenge, as I wanted to prove myself. I took the key chain they gave me and, after trying several keys, I was able to start the scooter. As I was riding along on the scooter I was stopped by a policeman. Being fearful of what might happen to me if the truth were to come to light, I lied to the policeman, telling him that the scooter belonged to my father.

On another occasion, I became embroiled in an argument with my next-door neighbor over his daughter. This neighbor happened to be a highly respected engineer who also had two sons. The family belonged to the Vaisya caste, so my relationship with this girl was not going to work anyway. But I kept on approaching her despite the fact that her family disapproved of my seeing her. On one occasion, when I was spending time at the girl's house, a confrontation ensued. The father started an argument with me and I pushed him. The police got involved in trying to defuse the situation.

I was escorted to the police station and was forced to sit on a bench in the lobby. Since I belonged to the Brahmin caste and my family was well respected in the community, no record of the incident was made. My brother, Sudhakar, who had a lot of connections with people in high places within the community, relied on his good name as well as that of the family to clear up the situation.

Despite this rather troubling period in my life, I did not try to escape my problems by turning to alcohol or drugs, nor did I take up smoking. During this time, I also continued to study and gain increased knowledge about the many Hindu gods and goddesses. Although I had a lot of hurt on the inside, I was acting religiously and I presented an outward appearance of being spiritual. However, I had to mask my inward feelings since I was a Brahmin.

My parents were quite concerned about my future, especially since there was so much turmoil going on in my life. Not knowing what to do, they consulted with a couple of scholarly Brahmin priests who were experts in interpreting horoscopes as well as the holy writings. These priests suggested that I should undergo a specific religious ceremony in order to release me from any curses related to bad luck. This ceremony involved interaction with the monkey god, Hanuman. I had to get up early in the morning, bathe in cold water, put on clean clothes, and then visit any temple in which Hanuman was the main god.

After reaching this temple, I had to walk around the inside of it 105 times, all the while continuously chanting this god's name, Hanuman. This ritual was repeated for forty consecutive days. In support of my fulfilling the individual tasks associated with this ritual, my father voluntarily took me to this temple each morning. I fulfilled these tasks in order to win the approval of my parents, bring me good luck, and gain the protection of this god against any possible harm or danger.

In addition to this ritual, I also stood on one foot for as long as I could in hopes of gaining the approval of one of the many Hindu gods. I practiced this ritual alone in secret. My family was not even aware that I was performing this ritual on my own without prompting. I believed that by performing this ritual I would somehow gain extra protection and might even score some extra points in terms of gaining the approval of some of the Hindu gods.

Furthermore, each time that I messed up and wronged someone, I performed some good deed in hopes that the good I did would somehow outweigh the bad. But while practicing these rituals, never once did I accept personal responsibility for any of my wrong doings. Even though I already have a great deal of knowledge about these many Hindu gods, I still maintained an interest in increasing my knowledge about them. Deep down within myself, I wanted to be someone of importance from a spiritual standpoint.

During this period in my life I lost interest in school and furthering my education. My grades declined and I began to suffer emotionally. Since my father was an educator, I was obligated to become highly educated. More importantly, it was my duty to pursue a secondary education in order to be considered a good Brahmin. Two things come to mind when I think of an acceptable career for a Brahmin—becoming either a priest or an academician. Since I had already lost interest in academics, the only choice left for me was to pursue the possibility of becoming a Hindu priest. Thus, while failing in school, I continued to gain a lot of head knowledge concerning spiritual and religious aspects related to the Hindu religion.

My hunger to learn more about other religions and spiritual matters further motivated me to study and gain a great deal of knowledge on mythology, especially in relation to gods and goddesses and their powers, limitations, and character. The study of these gods was not only thought provoking but very demanding. It would be completely understandable for an individual to study for years and even attain a degree in Hinduism and still not be able to understand all aspects related to the many deities.

As early as the age of ten or eleven years, I began to pay special attention to the Hindu deities, the holy writings, and the sacred texts. Thus early on I gained an in-depth knowledge about many Hindu gods and goddesses, which further spurred my desire to study certain sacred holy writings such as the Vedas, the Upanishads, the Puranas, the Ramayana, the Mahabharatha, and the famous Bhagawad-Gita.

Two of the favorite epics that I enjoyed reading included Ramayana and Mahabharatha. According to these writings, Lord Rama is the seventh avatar and Lord Krishna is the eighth avatar of Lord Vishnu. The Bhagawad-Gita, otherwise known as "god's song," is part of the great epic known as Mahabharatha.

CHAPTER 5

EMOTIONAL STRUGGLES

BEING MUCH LOVED, overly pampered, and spoiled are just some of the many privileges that the youngest child of an Indian family has bestowed on him. But this position also has some drawbacks. As the youngest child, I had to obey and follow what I was being told without a say in the matter most times. Even though I was loved and accepted just as much as any other of my siblings, I did not always receive the same respect or standing when dealing with important issues of life; my opinions were not valued or respected.

Over the years, I observed two things that seemed rather odd and unfair. First, in many Hindu families, mine included, it is not customary for the older siblings to approach the younger ones, in particular the youngest sibling, to ask for their opinion, advice, suggestion, or feedback. Secondly, it is also not customary for the eldest siblings to offer their apologies to a younger sibling, especially when that sibling happens to be the youngest.

For example, I do not recall a single incident or circumstance in which I was asked to forgive another sibling's wrongdoing. It doesn't seem likely to me that my siblings were always right and I was always wrong. Perhaps a feeling of self-righteousness or false pride was the underlying cause for their seeming inability to admit to making an error or having any shortcomings.

Rather than admit to any weaknesses, they chose instead not to humble themselves, nor to say that they were sorry. The Bible instructs followers of Christ to do the opposite. The second chapter of the book of Philippians says, "Let nothing be done through strife or vainglory; but in lowliness of mind let each one esteem other better than themselves" (Phil. 2:3, 4, KJV).

Although I admit that I am far from being perfect—and the Lord knows that I have my share of wrongdoings—I strongly believe that no person is right or wrong 100% of the time. Furthermore, every human being, including myself, has both strengths and weaknesses. Expecting me to constantly apologize to every one of my siblings was a very frustrating experience. It also caused me to have doubts about my character or personality. So I began to act out my frustrations by rebelling.

During this troubling period in my life I was skipping classes and doing many things that were not pleasing to my family, as well as to the various Hindu gods. But I was at a loss as to how I could handle the emotional turmoil that I felt or what I should do to nullify these feelings. In the meantime, I was slowly and surely becoming very self-centered and was doing just about whatever pleased me, all the while not caring about whom I might be hurting. My carefree self-centered lifestyle resulted in my failing the 7th, 10th, and 12th grades at school.

These failures made me feel as though I was fighting a losing battle, as my life seemed to be spiraling out of control. Because I was a Brahmin, I felt uneasy confessing or owning up to all of my inner feelings and exposing all of my shortcomings. I guess that I was secretly hoping that somehow, with time, these feelings would just all go away. But as time passed, my problems seemed to be increasing rather than decreasing.

I suppose that I could have agreed to the option of seeing a counselor. But in general, and especially among many Brahmin families, it is not considered customary to expose the weaknesses of any family member since these shortcomings may negatively affect the perception that others have of the entire family. Thus I chose not to open up and confess all of my feelings. I also did not want to be ridiculed or rejected because of these shortcomings just so that I could be honest about having them.

Nevertheless, I was hoping that I would be accepted without being questioned. All along, deep down inside, I knew that I could not live too long like this without coming to some kind of resolution in terms of my shortcomings. I found that I was increasingly seeking or turning towards the gods for my protection.

During my teenage years, I faced many problems both while at home and at school. It was especially difficult for me to understand why I was being given so much unconditional love at home, yet I felt like I was a disappointment to my family. From a spiritual standpoint, I was at a loss to explain why I was having such difficulties.

On a human level, I speculated that the root causes of most of my problems stemmed from the choices I made, my emotional instability and immaturity, my having embraced a self-centered rebellious lifestyle, personality traits such as being extremely stubborn, and my ignorance.

In my early years while practicing Hinduism, I was living my life to the fullest but in a twisted manner, savoring each moment as long as the end result was pleasing to me. I unabashedly said whatever was on my mind without taking into account those whom I might be hurting or the consequences of my hurtful words. It seemed that my family paid the price in terms of consequences during my childhood, but later on in life I also reaped the consequences of my actions.

A long time passed before I realized the potential impact or consequences that might come about as a direct result of my thoughts, actions, deeds, motives, and desires. Nonetheless, in light of God's Word, every individual must face and accept the consequences associated with their thoughts and deeds, and there is no escape, at least in terms of one's accountability before God.

The Scripture says, "Be not deceived; God is not mocked; for whatsoever a man soweth, that shall he also reap" (Gal. 6:7, KJV).

As a victim of my own ignorance and self-deception, I will be the first one to acknowledge a deeper sense of what the apostle Paul was teaching in regard to this Scripture.

The head knowledge that I had gained about many Hindu gods was just that to me, and nothing more. It seemed that all the head knowledge that I gained during my years of study about these gods did not fill the void within me or give me any satisfaction in terms of having a personal relationship with any of them. I also began to experience a great deal of confusion and was feeling very lonely.

During my search for truth, it became apparent to me that I was spiritually lost. I did not feel that I was being respected. Furthermore, all the accumulated knowledge that I possessed about the gods was not helping to bring about the respect that I so desperately desired. During this time of hardship, out of desperation I turned for help to my favorite gods as well as those I feared. Secretly, I was hoping that one of them would bail me out.

Furthermore, I believed that I could rely on all my good deeds, such as prayers, reading the sacred texts, fasting, and participation in rituals to replace what I yearned for, such as love, compassion, mercy, and forgiveness. But each time that I would share my spiritual confusion with someone of importance and request their advice in the matter, their response always seemed to be general in nature. For example, they would say, "Just pray about it and let it go." But I really needed to hear something like, "God will listen to your cry."

Failure to get the kind of support that I was looking for left me feeling disappointed, lonely, rejected, and eventually depressed. Deep inside, I knew that I was not living a life that was pleasing to the gods. Yet I lived in denial in this regard. In general, it is not easy for Brahmins to admit to having any weaknesses or shortcomings. This is especially true since others are expected to look up to them with much respect because of their high status.

It was during this time that I also began pushing away those who were closest to me. I began to take on a persona that made it difficult for others to love and accept me. These changes were mainly due to the disillusionment that I came away with when I failed to gain a one-on-one relationship with any of the gods that I had so fully embraced with my trust, especially Lord Hanuman (the monkey god) and Lord Ganesha.

My parents became very concerned about my future, so much so that they once again consulted a couple of Brahmin priests who were experts in their field. These priests were well versed in terms of the scriptures and possessed an in-depth knowledge on how to predict an individual's past, present, and possibly future, by reading hands and horoscopes. They did so by studying the zodiac signs and stars in relation to an individual's time of birth. One of the priests even went so far as to tell my parents that I was going to experience a great deal of bad luck for at least nineteen years and another one estimated this period of bad luck to last for at least twenty-one years, and possibly even longer.

According to these priests, all this bad luck was linked to my karma, also known as my destiny. Thus I was at a loss in terms of turning things around. The only recourse I had was to accept things as they were and endure the consequences. This kind of thinking agrees with an age-old Hindu saying that states no one can escape the plans set forth by Lord Brahma (also known as Brahma Raatha in the Telugu language). The literal meaning of raatha is *writing*. In other words, Lord Brahma has already planned everyone's destiny. No one can change his or her destiny, as it is not acceptable for an individual to refuse or reject their karma. Furthermore, it is not possible to do so since Lord Brahma has already decided an individual's karma. Most Hindus accept this belief, that is, whatever has been predestined will come to pass and there are absolutely no ifs, ands, or buts about it. A person has no authority to ask any questions or challenge this kind of thinking.

According to the belief that everyone has an assigned karma, there is no room to bargain or negotiate in terms of an individual's destiny since it is all in the god's hands. From a Christian stand-point, individuals do not have to worry or fear about karma, or for that matter any other generational curses. For example, when an individual accepts Jesus Christ as his or her personal Lord and Savior, that person begins life anew. No longer does that person have to be concerned about the past, present, or future. The Scripture that supports this thinking is, "If anyone is in Christ, he is a new creation; old things have passed away; behold, all things have become new" (2 Cor. 5:17, NKJV).

My acceptance of the belief about having an assigned karma, one for which I would have to suffer and endure some period of hard times for up to twenty-one years or longer, caused me to become very frustrated and disappointed in terms of having any hope for my future. This type of thinking does not allow for a belief in forgiveness. As Christians, if we have done something to bring on a time of judgment by God, all we need to do is go to God, repent, and ask for His forgiveness. He will give us a clean slate in terms of any wrongdoing; He throws the incident into the sea of forgetfulness. The beauty of this is that individuals can simply approach Jesus just as they are and be assured that He will accept them. Furthermore, once the incident is forgiven it is as though the transgression had never even occurred.

The hardships that I endured early on in life left me with distant feelings towards God. I had not yet experienced a one-on-one personal relationship with Him, despite my having a strong desire for this type of relationship. Furthermore, up to this point in my life I had never felt that God loved me or desired to have a personal relationship with me. At that time in my life, I was failing to fulfill my heart's desires while worshiping and fervently praying to my favorite Hindu gods.

Although my parents and siblings gave me a lot of unconditional love, I still felt very lost, confused, and lonely from a spiritual standpoint. Deep within me, I was beginning to realize that I was just going through the motions in a ritualistic manner, in terms of living my life. Although I was dissatisfied with my life on the whole, I did not dare to walk away from it only because the opportunity to do so did not present itself. It was at that time that my parents agreed to send me to live with my eldest brother in the United States. They hoped that going there would afford me better opportunities in which to pursue a higher education. But they also hoped that a change of venue might help me to make some positive, productive changes from both an emotional and a spiritual standpoint. My eldest brother agreed to have me live with his family for a couple of years, at least until I finished a college associate degree.

My whole family agreed that a change in environment might do me some good. I remember being very happy and excited about having the opportunity to come to live in the United States. To me, the plan represented a chance for a newfound freedom to study and to choose what I believed without any restriction or reservations.

CHAPTER 6

COMING TO THE UNITED STATES

IN ORDER TO come to the United States on a student visa (also referred to as an F-1 Visa), I had to have a sponsor or a letter of acceptance from a college in the United States. My eldest brother, who lives in Michigan, had already received his citizenship from the United States, and he agreed to sponsor me. This was not an easy task; securing a student visa was very difficult to begin with, but especially in my case because I had failed so many grades while attending school in India.

My brother prepared all the required sponsorship and immigration documentation and mailed the paperwork to our house in India. In order to apply for a student visa, I was required to visit one of the American Consulate General's offices in India. I chose to visit the one located in Madras (now called Chennai) since it was only a day's journey from my hometown of Hyderabad.

After arriving there, I encountered a lot of difficulties. Due to my past record of academic failures, I was assigned to talk with a representative who specialized in helping clients with an especially difficult situation. This representative informed me that an American officer would interview me concerning my request for the student visa. This officer interviewed me and then informed me that he was denying my request. Evidently he was concerned that

I would continue to fail academically after coming to the United States. This would not only bring to bear a bad name on my family in India but also to the college that I would be attending.

This denial left me feeling very rejected; I became extremely depressed and isolated myself from both my friends and family. My mother suggested that I should seriously consider praying to the second male god V (Lord Venkateswara) and then promise him that if he would help me secure a student visa, I would do something in his honor. I took my mother's advice, and prayed, asking god V to help me secure a student visa. In return, I promised that the next time that I visited India, I would climb all 5,000 steps going up the seven levels of hills leading to the temple that was dedicated to the god V. This temple was built at a high altitude and was located in a place known as Tirupathi, which is a day's journey from Hyderabad. The single-lane road going up each of these hills is narrow, allowing only one vehicle heading in each direction.

I was afraid of this god. I had heard that when an individual makes a promise to this particular god and fails to fulfill it, the person should expect something bad to happen either at that time or later on. I also had heard and read many stories involving supernatural events in association with this god. As I recall, there was one such incident in which a young man was praying to this god for a certain blessing. In return for an answer to his prayer, he made a promise. After receiving the blessing, he failed to make good on his word. Later, when he was flying a kite on the roof of a two- story building, he fell onto the cement below and broke his leg. He had many years of experience flying a kite while on top of this particular roof without incident. Thus the cause of this incident was attributed to consequences associated with his failed promise.

A few months after I had prayed to god V about getting my request for a student visa making my promise, I once again visited the American consulate for another try at obtaining a student visa. The same officer who had originally denied my request interviewed me again. Much to my surprise, he remembered me and said, "It's you again." I asked him to give me about three minutes to further explain myself before making another decision in regards to my request. Basically, I told him that the reason for my having a poor academic record was due to my having gone through a rough period of bad luck for quite a long time. Due to all this bad luck, I first started to rebel, then made some bad choices in what I did as well as in terms of my choice of friends. These bad choices then led to bad consequences, and eventually I lost interest in my education. At the same time, I was also getting very confused and felt lost in terms of my walk with the gods. I was becoming increasingly confused about whether or not I was pleasing these gods or just plain making them angry.

I pleaded with the officer to be kind enough to just give me one more chance to turn my situation around by approving my request for this visa. I told him I felt confident that if I was allowed to go abroad I would be able to change my life for the better, and that I would be very appreciative for his assistance in helping me to gain this visa. Once I had presented my case, he told me that he needed a couple of hours to think about it. He requested that I return to see him at that window around 4:00 pm that same day. I remember feeling anxious. When the time came for me to see the officer and my name was called, to my astonishment my application for a student visa was approved. It meant that soon I would be on my way to the United States.

Before I left India, my mother reminded me of the promise that I had made to god V. I told her that I was planning on keeping my promise. But it was with some trepidation and great anticipation that I left India. To this day though, I still don't know the specifics as to how my application for a student visa finally got approved. Once again, God—the true God—works in mysterious ways.

Some people thought that my visa was approved because of my response and genuine tone of voice in what I said during my second visit. Others insisted that it only got approved because god V intervened on my behalf and influenced others to turn the situation around in my favor. By the time I visited India again in 1987, I had already become a Christian. I no longer believed that other gods had an influence over the events of my life, so I did not keep my promise to god V. This greatly concerned my parents but they chose not to pressure me about it since I had made it clear to them that I would no longer bow down or pray to any of the Hindu gods. I told my family that the Bible states, "you shall have no other gods before Me" (Ex. 20:3, NKJV). I also shared with them what was said in the book of Second Corinthians, "Old things have passed away, behold, all things have become new" (2 Cor. 5:17, NKJV).

In the fall of 1982, I came to the United States to live with my brother, sister-in-law, and their two children. I started my studies working toward an associate degree in business administration at a local community college in Michigan. In the beginning, on many levels, I found living in the United States to be very challenging. First, it was a new environment and I had no friends. Second, I found the language difficult to understand. I had been taught the English language in India but, compared to India, the use of slang and colloquialisms were more common in the United States. Third, I had a great deal of homesickness. Furthermore, at that time I was not aware of any temples in Michigan that I could visit and, not wanting to burden those around me, I felt as though I had to keep the things that bothered me to myself. Despite the love, affection, and understanding that my brother and his family were giving me, I still felt lonely, lost, and confused.

I had the desire to read and do research on other faiths and beliefs, but did not do so at that time because I was unsure of what consequences I might face. Thus, I placed all of these desires on hold for the time being. Shortly after earning a two-year associate degree in business administration, I transferred to Central Michigan University to continue my undergraduate education.

CHAPTER 7

SEEKING AND SEARCHING THE TRUTH

WHILE STUDYING AT Central Michigan University, I immediately started doing my own study and research on other major world religions. I began to make friends with individuals of other religious faiths from other countries. Right before I started to investigate as to whom God was, I said a simple prayer: "Dear God, I may have some head knowledge, but I don't really know you personally. Whoever you are, please reveal yourself to me and I will promise to keep an open mind and maintain a childlike faith. I only want to know and find the truth and I will not settle for anything less."

Based solely on the sincerity of that prayer, I began an intense, in-depth search for truth as it relates to God. I first decided to study the Qur'an, as I had recently made friends with some Muslims on campus. I took notes while studying this book and asked my Muslim friends many questions in terms of their faith. Slowly but surely I gained a lot of knowledge about Islam, especially in terms of what Muslims believed and taught. I already had gained some life-experience knowledge about Islam while living in India. I had attended a school that was attended predominantly by Muslims and had made friends with a lot of them. At that time, approximately

10 percent of India's population was Muslim so I had met Muslims in my own neighborhood in my hometown of Hyderabad.

A study of the Qur'an and the Muslim faith was next followed by reading and researching other Eastern religions, including Buddhism, Taoism, Shintoism, Zen, Confucianism, Zoroastrianism, Jainism, Sikhism, and Bahai. I also investigated Judaism and Christianity.

As I was reading the beliefs and faiths of each of these religions, I made a chart that included information on each religion that would allow me to compare important aspects of each one. For example, I charted information on such topics as who God is, the founder, the ability to love and accept us just as we are, what they teach about heaven, hell, the afterlife, humanity, the sin factor, salvation, and sacred texts.

While conducting this in-depth study and searching for the truth as it relates to God, I remember meeting a man of God, a Christian preacher. Being a preacher, he wanted to share his faith (the gospel) with me. He also wanted me to receive salvation by becoming a born-again believer or genuine Christian.

Although he was eager to share his beliefs, he never once showed any interest in what I believed. I made it clear to him that I was a Hindu and that I too was interested in sharing my beliefs with others. I told him that in the name of communication each individual has to speak as well as listen to the others person's opinions and that it was only fair and right to do so. I made an appointment to meet with this preacher in the cafeteria one week after our initial meeting.

During the week before our meeting, we had agreed to study each other's faith so that when we met for our appointment we would be prepared to exchange information on our questions, concerns, and curiosities. When I showed up for our appointment one week later, he failed to show. During the week before this appointment, I studied the gospels in the Bible. Much to my surprise, I was taken aback by what I was reading, especially concerning what I was reading about Jesus Christ.

A few days later I again ran into this preacher, and when I confronted him about our missed meeting, he came up with an excuse. But I could tell that he did not want to read anything about the Hindu beliefs or about other individual's beliefs or religions. I challenged him by telling him that if he was really a strong and true believer of the gospel, he did not have to be afraid of anything. The example that I related to him was that just walking into a garage did not make an individual become an automobile any more than walking into a temple made an individual a Hindu.

Having the preacher not show up for our appointment made me feel a little uncomfortable, and I immediately judged Christians as being too narrow minded and decided not to let anyone preach or witness to me from that point on. When the preacher found out that I was maintaining a distance from him and other Christian individuals, he suggested that I watch Christian programs on the television in order to learn about the Christian faith. I liked that idea and began to watch a few Christian programs, especially the 700 Club hosted by Dr. Pat Robertson.

At the same time that I was watching the 700 Club, I was still very much interested in investigating other religious beliefs in my quest to search and seek for the truth. During this search, I began to ask myself many questions that may have seemed illogical at the time. But these questions helped to raise my curiosity and helped me to keep an open mind to information that could possibly point me in a direction to which I was not accustomed. The questions that I was pondering included the following:

1. Am I fully convinced that my way, the Hindu way, is the only way?
2. Am I being rude and disrespectful when I tell others that what they believe is wrong?
3. If I am a good person, why would a loving God send me to hell?
4. As in the old expression, "all roads lead to Rome," do all religions lead to God?

5. Why do Christians profess and proclaim that the Bible has all the answers one needs.
6. 6. Why does one need to accept Jesus Christ in order to be saved from eternal damnation?
7. Why should anyone try to convince or even force his beliefs on others, especially when it is not being requested?
8. What is the meaning of life and what role does God want me to play in the great scheme of life?

With these and several other questions in mind, I was determined to pursue my investigation at any cost so that I could gain peace of mind. At the same time, I also wanted to be able to find the truth so that I could share my findings with others. These factors formed the basis for my motivation to continue my study of other faiths.

CHAPTER 8

WHY LEARN ABOUT OTHER FAITHS?

BEFORE UNDERSTANDING OTHER religions or belief systems, I first defined the meaning of the term religion. The Oxford Desk Dictionary defines religion as a "belief in a personal God or gods entitled to obedience and worship; expression of this in worship; particular systems of faith and worship and thing that one is devoted to."

I believe that it is very important for a genuine child of God to educate himself not only in the Bible, but also in other religions or belief systems. The Bible strongly supports this statement and declares that, "My people are destroyed for lack of knowledge" (Hos. 4:6, NKJV). I believe that this Scripture not only applies to an in-depth knowledge of the Bible but also to other religions or belief systems. I believe that the apostle Paul also held this view when he stated that, "I have become all things to all men, that I might by all means save some" (1 Cor. 9:22, NKJV).

Why should individuals study religions and why should it matter whether or not they do this anyway? I believe they should do this because many individuals need something to turn to for strength during times of need or distress. For example, many politicians as well as many others united together and turned to prayer when the events of 9-11-01 took place in New York City.

In doing so, they surely hoped to gain strength and draw comfort from uniting with one another and to rise up against a threat. They sought for a common cause to protect our liberty.

Is it necessary for individuals to learn the truth about other religions? The answer is a resounding "yes." While reading a well-known Christian author Gerald McDermott's book *Can Evangelicals Learn from World Religions?* I thought about four reasons why we should learn about other religions or belief systems:

1. In order to become more sensitive to what other people believe.
2. Learning about other belief systems helps us to appreciate our own faith more.
3. Learning about other religions will give us compassion for other people.
4. Knowing what other people believe will show us that God is at work in more ways, lands, and people than many of us had imagined.

When revisiting the original question of, does religion matter, the answer I found, once again, is a resounding "yes." This is true because most individuals need something that they can believe in. Many people have used the statement, "If we don't stand for something, we will fall for anything." This statement contains a great deal of truth since individuals face many temptations on a daily basis. If we are weak and unstable, we are especially at risk of succumbing to these temptations.

Of course there are those who profess to be atheists, agnostics, secular humanists, or followers of various new age beliefs and may not necessarily be asking, does religion or God matter? Furthermore, there are always exceptions to the rule. Because of the freedom, liberty, and freewill that we enjoy in America, not everyone agrees with everything that we believe. And many of us are so concerned and preoccupied with our own selfish or self-centered desires that we may overlook associated consequences.

I was reading the book *Guide to Cults, Religions, and Spiritual Beliefs* by Bruce Bickel and Stan Jantz. They point out a very interesting comment. Many of us assume that people who hold other beliefs are completely in the dark. In my opinion, many believers are guilty of this as well, due to either ignorance or narrow-mindedness. By thinking this way we risk alienating others from wanting to know more about our faith.

The apostle Paul chose to address this issue in a more subtle manner. Addressing the foolishness of Greeks, Paul said, "We preach Christ crucified, to the Jews a stumbling block and to the Gentiles foolishness" (1 Cor. 1:22, NKJV). A Greek of Paul's day may not have considered himself to be foolish because he did not believe that God can save people through Christ. But the underlying truth here is that our finite minds cannot grasp or comprehend the supernatural things of God unless the Holy Spirit reveals the truth to us. We are not always on the same wavelength as God. The Lord Himself declared this in the book of Isaiah when He said, "My thoughts are not your thoughts, nor are your ways my ways" (Isa. 55:8, NKJV).

The apostle Paul further elaborated on this issue when he wrote, "But the natural man receiveth not the things of the Spirit of God: for they are foolishness unto him: neither can he know them, because they are spiritually discerned. But he that is spiritual judgeth all things, yet he himself is judged of no man. For who hath known the mind of the Lord, that he may instruct him?" (1 Cor. 2:14–16).

In keeping with His very nature, God can survive on His own. He does not need human interaction even though He desires to have a personal one-on-one relationship with each of us. The Bible declares that God made us in His own image. On the other hand, humans cannot survive without God. We need Him and His fellowship.

We are subject to God's reasoning but He is not subject to our reasoning. Thus He does not owe us any explanation about who He is. And yet He desires to reason with us as we read in the first chapter of the book of Isaiah: "'Come now, and let us reason together,' says the Lord, 'Though your sins are like scarlet, they shall be as white as snow; Though they are red like crimson, they shall be as wool'" (Isa.1:18, NKJV).

As finite beings with only limited knowledge, we need something bigger than ourselves to believe in and be part of. We need to know what we believe and why we believe what we believe or don't believe. In other words, we need to know where we stand in terms of our beliefs and, in the process, we need to search for and establish our true spiritual identity. It is important for us to know and understand who we are, why we are here, the roles that we must play, and the reason for our existence.

I believe that God created us for a purpose and that He has a plan for each one of us. The best way that we can find out His plan for us is to know Him and to partner with Him. In order to know and understand God's purpose for our lives, it is imperative that we build a one-on-one personal relationship with Him.

One of the best things that God blessed us with is a conscience. Having a conscience enables us to be able to differentiate right from wrong. It also enables us to be able to distinguish truth from untruth. God desires that we use our conscience as a measuring tool, not only when it comes to speaking the truth but also as it applies to living it out.

Our conscience tells us when we fail to live up to God's holy standards. In terms of speaking the truth, a well-known Christian author once said, "While we may acknowledge, appreciate, and even respect the truth found in other religions, that does not mean that those religions contain saving truth or a truth that leads to salvation" (Halverson, 2003).

With so many religions in existence, it is possible for an individual to get confused, not to mention even face an unsettling fear of uncertainty of the unknown. On the one hand, there seems to be a vast amount of information available at our fingertips about each religion, yet, conversely, there seems to be lot of pressure on us to obey and follow the religion which our parents and their predecessors followed and have passed on to us. We are then expected to walk in their footsteps.

Almost all religions teach or share some similar beliefs such as to love one another, help the poor and needy, or honor our parents. But, these religions differ on important aspects such as who God is, who Jesus is, the salvation process, and the afterlife. With so much confusion abounding, it is essential that we ask ourselves one very important question: "What is the truth?" We must all sincerely and diligently seek for the truth as it relates to God and, once we find out what that truth is, we must sincerely embrace it and apply it to our lives on a daily basis.

One author explains that Christianity is the only religion where God is really God. It's the only one where God saves people instead of the people trying to save themselves. This aspect alone was one of the many features of Christianity that drew me to study this faith. The crucifixion and resurrection of Christ were the two events in the Bible that appealed to me the most.

CONCLUSION AND FINAL NOTE

BASED ON WHAT has been presented and explained here, one can see that there are so many gods and goddesses to choose from that we may not know if we will be offending any. For instance, most Hindus (if not all) revere and fear Lord Ganesha. When one does not put this god first, there could be some serious consequences. Then there is the goddess Kali whom lots of people tend to fear as well. Then there is Lord V whom many worship as well as fear.

People have to come to grips with reality as to which god or goddess they should choose to pray to and worship, or which god or goddess they should pick to be more important than others. There seems to be lot of confusion about religious beliefs, not to mention contradictions. Of the many issues in Hinduism that I have trouble with, the one that bothers me the most, is that man (though very sinful in nature) is sometimes seen to be equal to God and possibly more than God in some special cases, as we can read in the Vedas and Upanishads.

While I was reading the Bible, the vast differences between Hinduism and Christianity became strikingly apparent to me. The reasons I left Hinduism are many: I was feeling spiritually helpless and hopeless, not to mention lost, confused, and lonely. There was a big spiritual void in me. I was getting tired of always having to depend on works in order to escape from the vicious cycles of samsara.

As a Hindu, I had no say as to who I was in the previous lifetime(s) and, above all, no one could even tell me who I would be in future lifetimes. I was not even sure if I was going to heaven or hell. It all depended on my karma. I had enough problems dealing and accepting with fixed karma much less good and bad karma. I am glad to know that in the Bible, God shows us His mercy and grace. Having to prove ourselves based on works is just not necessary in order to be saved.

SECTION TWO

HINDUISM: THAT OLD TIME RELIGION

CHAPTER 9

WHO IS A HINDU?

A HINDU IS a person who adheres to Hinduism, the religion that is followed by the vast majority of people in India. In this religion, the focus is placed more on what one does as opposed to what one thinks. As one author aptly stated, "Each individual follows a way of life that provides some meaning to it. One comes across many improvisations in Hindu homes" (Bhalla, 2007).

In general, the Hindu way of life is based on the teachings found in the Vedas. The teachings found in the Upanishads have also had an influence on this way of life. Self or personal realization is the main focus of the Upanishads. Over time, Hindus have also been turning to such practices and beliefs as meditation, yoga, reincarnation, and existence of the soul, also referred to as Atman.

Based on this change in thinking, a Hindu is now allowed to believe in everlasting life; that is, one does not die, and, therefore, one's soul does not experience death. Furthermore, with this thinking, although the physical body dies, the soul lives on and ultimately gets transferred into another body. Bhalla points out that "the selection of a body depends upon actions performed in a lifetime."

Influences on Hinduism have evolved over time. It was first influenced by the Vedas, and then by the Upanishads. Currently, the Puranas have begun to exert the greatest influence on the Hindu way of life. The Puranas contain the two great epics known as the *Ramayana* and *Mahabharatha*. These two epics have become great sources of inspiration, so much so that they have been made into movies, as well as into television serials. In doing so, they have become readily recognized amongst Indian households.

Hinduism is the third most popular religion in the world, trailing just behind Christianity and Islam. It is estimated that approximately 13 percent of the world's population and about 81 percent of India's population are Hindus. Thus, one out of every six people on earth is a Hindu. According to one author, "There are more than 60 million Hindus living outside India and over a million of them live in North America" (Johnsen, 2002).

Hinduism does not have a definite date for its inception, and there is also no single founder or prophet who has been identified as its founder. But early on, many different dates for its inception were proposed. Whatever the case may be, the closest date that many authors seem to agree upon is somewhere around 4,000 years before Christ. Len Woods, in his book *Handbook of World Religions*, states that "The Dravidians of the Mohenjo-Daro civilization were overrun by the more aggressive Aryan peoples from ancient Persia, also known as modern day Iran. The amalgamation of the cultures that practiced polytheism and animism provided the basis for what eventually developed into Hinduism." The basic premise of Hinduism is that God is all and all is God. This premise is considered to be pantheistic because pan means *all* and theism means *God*.

Answering the question "What is Hinduism?" is not an easy task because people view or perceive Hinduism in their own ways. Hinduism can mean different things to different people. For example, some Hindus think that one can understand Hinduism just by reading and becoming familiar with the Vedas. Others think that it is imperative to know just the Upanishads. Others believe it is important to understand only the Puranas, and to yet another group believes it is important to understand only the two great epics of Ramayana and Mahabharatha. Since Hinduism is so tolerant of other beliefs, in one sense one can come to understand it by relying upon whatever one chooses to believe. But the problem that one may encounter with this kind of thinking is that there may not be a single notion upon which everyone can agree.

In contrast, those who choose to believe in the Bible must adhere to what it states, and there is no room for individual interpretation. Either a person accepts the entire Bible as the Word of God or he doesn't. Thus, in terms of the Bible, we don't have the option of picking or choosing what we can believe.

Hinduism is difficult to define, as it is much more than a religion; it is a way of life. Its roots can be traced back to around 3,000 years before Christ (a different version of the date) during the time in which the famous and well-known Indus Valley Civilization was in existence. The phrase that comes to my mind when I think of Hinduism is "all is one or everything is one." In terms of its foundation, one author states that "It has no beginning, no founder, no central authority, no hierarchy, and no organization" (Pollock, 2002).

As mentioned earlier, no prophet or any significant individual has been identified as the founder of Hinduism. Furthermore, no headquarters or holy city has been identified as being central in association with its practice. For example, Prophet Muhammad is credited as being the founder of Islam, Abraham is considered to be the father or founder of Judaism, and Jesus is credited as being the founder of Christianity. These three religions have certain sites that are considered to be holy. For example, Muslims recognize Mecca as the holy city, Christians and Jews recognize Jerusalem as the holy city, and Mormons recognize Salt Lake City as the holy city. Thus, Hinduism is a religion without any clear beginning or any single founder. Although different dates for the inception of Hinduism have been proposed, my research tends to support 4,000 years before Christ as being the closest approximation.

In their book *World Religions and Cults 101*, Christian authors Bickel and Jantz note that "Hinduism isn't even a single religion, but rather a collection of interwoven beliefs that can trace their roots back to the Hindu culture in India." They consider Hinduism as more or less a designer religion. It is also considered to be the world's oldest religion, mainly because it has no beginning and it has been said that it precedes recorded history.

The Himalayan Academy describes Hinduism as "a mystical religion, leading the devotee to personally experience the Truth within, finally reaching the pinnacle of consciousness where man and God are one." The academy further states that Hinduism has four main denominations: Saivism, Shaktism, Vaishnavism, and Smartism.

CHAPTER 10

THE BELIEF SYSTEM

HINDUISM IS CONSIDERED to be both the most open-minded as well as the most tolerant religion in the world today. Although its beliefs may disagree with certain beliefs of other religions, it maintains an accepting and understanding attitude toward other religions and faiths. One author explains the reason for this seeming tolerance is that "It is home for so many different people, cultures, religions, and languages" (Johnsen, 2002)

What one believes is important because it determines that individual's thoughts and attitudes about life in general and eventually directs that person's specific actions. Furthermore, some believe that our actions may set things into motion, which could possibly have an impact on our destiny. Our beliefs, especially about such things as God, heaven, and salvation are very important in terms of how we approach life. In general, Hindus believe in many diverse things, but there are certain core beliefs in which most Hindus seem to agree. These beliefs include the following:

1. A superior being who is both immanent and transcendent, someone who is creator but is not manifested as reality.
2. The divinity of the four Vedas, the ancient scriptures. The Agamas, as equally revealed, are espoused as God's words

put to song, the foundation of Sanatana Dharma, or eternal religion.

3. The universe, which undergoes repeating cycles of creation, preservation, and dissolution.

4. Karma, or the law of cause and effect, by which individuals create their own destiny by way of their thoughts and deeds.

5. Reincarnation of the soul, whereby an individual's soul is transferred many times into another body, evolving each time to a higher order until all karmas have been resolved and moksha, or liberation from the cycle of rebirth, has been attained.

6. Divine beings that exist in the unseen world. Communication with these devas and gods is attainable through temple worship, rituals, sacraments, and personal devotionals.

7. An enlightened master or satguru is required in order to know the Transcendent Absolute, as are personal discipline, good conduct, purification, pilgrimage, self-inquiry, meditation, and surrender to God.

8. All life is sacred. Thus it should be loved and revered. One should practice ahimsa (non-violence) in thought, word, and deed.

9. No one religion teaches the only way to salvation above all others. All genuine paths are facets of God's light, deserving tolerance and understanding.

Most churches and Christian organizations have a brochure for distribution purposes that outlines their beliefs and explains their doctrinal beliefs. This is done regardless of their particular denominational affiliation. But this is not the case with Hinduism. The authors of *The Penguin Dictionary of Religions* describe this situation as it relates to Hinduism: "Hinduism is not a unity, having no founder, no single creed, no single universally accepted scripture, no single moral code or theological system, not a single concept of god central to it. It is rather a tradition that embraces a wide variety of religious positions."

Thus Hinduism may best be described as a melting pot, ready and willing to accept and acknowledge almost anything that comes along. In addition to the above-mentioned beliefs, Hindus may also take into account dharma (ethics and duties), samsara (continuing cycle of birth, life, death, and rebirth), and yogas (paths or practices).

The main focus of Hinduism is the belief in Brahman (universal truth) and Vedas. These two are looked up to as being the underlying universal life force that encompasses and embodies existence. One author stated it this way: "According to Hindu scriptures, one's ignorance of the true nature of the self (atman) as one with Brahman is what traps one in the cycle of endless death and reincarnation (samsara). Thus, the highest goal of Hinduism is liberation (moksha) from the karmic cycle of death and rebirth" (Hancock, 1999). In contrast, the Bible states that "and as it is appointed for men to die once, but after this the judgment" (Heb. 9:27).

Karma

Karma is a Sanskrit term which means *actions*. But other words, such as "work," or "deed," also have been used as a substitute in place of the term Karma. One particular term that is somewhat related to Karma is "destiny," a word that I learned about as I was growing up. Regardless of the word being used, its meaning relates to the moral law of cause and effect.

Karma not only deals with the action but also with any consequential subsequent reactions. Karma plays a key role in a Hindu's life because it sends a message that there is a direct correlation between one's moral choices and one's quality of life. This reciprocal relationship is believed to not only affect the present life but also that of future lives.

Hinduism states that humanity's primary problem is that people do not recognize or acknowledge their divine nature. According to one Christian author, speaking about the beliefs of Hinduism and referring to the 'Law of Karma' speaks about Hindus as "We have forgotten that we are extended from Brahman and that we have mistakenly attached ourselves to the desires of our separate selves or egos, and, thereby, to the consequences of its actions" (Halverson, 2003).

When an individual speaks about karma, he should also pay close attention to the terms "samsara" (reincarnation) and "moksha" (liberation) since the meaning of all three of these terms are interconnected, and cannot be viewed separately. Karma deals with one's action, samsara deals with a chain of actions, and moksha deals with the subsequent consequential reaction. Thus, these three terms are linked or interconnected in a similar manner to that of Newton's third law of gravity, which states that "for every action, there is an equal and opposite reaction." In other words, when performing an action one can expect some consequential reaction. The basis for karma depends completely on this concept of action and reaction.

The law of karma is most similar to the concept found in biblical Scripture, which states that what we sow is what we reap. In regard to this issue, the Bible further states, "Be not deceived; God is not mocked: for whatsoever a man soweth, that shall he also reap" (Gal. 6:7, KJV). In terms of accountability for the things we say, think, and do, an individual may deceive himself and fool others but no one can deceive or fool God since He knows and sees everything.

A well-known Hindu author relates his view on how the law of karma operates when he said, "Karma embraces everything in the world of phenomena: physical, mental, and spiritual. All actions produce a reaction. All thought produces rethought. Feelings produce refeeling and that is why no one escapes this chain of action and reaction" (Somany, 2003).

There are two kinds of karma, namely good karma and bad karma. For example, when an individual lives a good life that is based on good karma, then that person can expect to lead a good rebirth. Conversely, when one lives a bad life that is based on bad karma, then that person can expect to lead a bad rebirth.

The law of karma teaches that each individual is born with certain inadequacies and imperfections but, at the same time, individuals also have the freedom to do away with these inadequacies and imperfections so that they can have a promising or somewhat perfect future. Karma makes it possible for an individual's physical, mental, and spiritual condition to be improvised.

Another component of karma involves a heavy emphasis on thoughts. The law of karma strongly relates that an individual should learn to purify his or her thoughts. Specifically, it states that positive thoughts bring forth positive results and negative thoughts bring forth negative results. This belief relates to the biblical Scriptures that speak of sowing and reaping.

A mind that consistently entertains and encourages negative thoughts is one that, sooner or later, is bound to degenerate. Once an individual's mind begins to degenerate, it poses a greater risk for harming himself as opposed to others. Albert Einstein once said that a "mind is a terrible thing to waste."

Thoughts do not always die in vain. But all thoughts are associated with potential consequences and, oftentimes, they lead to actions. In other words, in order to take an action, one has to first encourage and entertain a thought. Thus it is reasonable to assume that there is no such thing as an action apart from a thought. A famous French philosopher, René Descartes, once stated that "I think, therefore I am."

The Bible examines the issue of our thoughts in depth and states that "as he thinketh in his heart, so is he" (Prov. 23:7). Jesus personally dealt with the topic of positive thinking when He said, "Love your enemies, bless them that curse you, do good to them that hate you, and pray for them which despitefully use you, and persecute you" (Matt.5:44).

Furthermore, the apostle Paul encourages us to follow this good advice: "whatsoever things are true, whatsoever things are honest, whatsoever things are just, whatsoever things are pure, whatsoever things are lovely, whatsoever things are of good report; if there be any virtue, and if there be any praise, think on these things" (Phil. 4:8, kjv). Having said all this, I have come to the realization that we should be careful about how and what we think, and we must try our best to bring our thoughts under subjection to the Word of God.

There are four types of karma; namely, "sanchita" karma, "prarabdha" karma, "kriyamana" karma, and "agama" karma. Sanchita karma is the sum total of an individual's past karmas that are yet to be resolved. Prarabdha karma is the part of sanchita karma that individuals experience in this life. Kriyamana karma deals with the actions that humans are currently producing but which will bear its fruit in the future. And finally, agama karma focuses on our plans for the future (where we are yet to act) and it is influenced by our thoughts.

The author of the book *The Complete Idiot's Guide to Hinduism,* describes these four karmas as follows:

> Sanchita karma is all the debits and credits in our soul's entire karmic portfolio. Prarabdha karma is the debits and credits we have to deal with during this incarnation. Kriyamana karma is the store of merits and demerits that we're currently adding to or subtracting from our karmic credit account. Agama karma is a more subtle type of karma. This type is produced not by any actions that an individual has done, but rather by their intentions to commit an action in the future.
>
> —Johnsen, 2002

There is also a type of karma known as fixed karma. Some of the incidents that have taken place in my life fit into this category, since this type of karma can be altered or changed only by God himself. Thus there is nothing that human beings can do to negate this type of karma on their own. In other words, the individual is at the mercy of a particular god in terms of having any influence on changing a particular karma.

Reincarnation

Reincarnation is central to the Hindu faith. It is accepted by almost everyone in India who identifies with this faith. Reincarnation explains the "death-birth cycle" and is also referred to as "transmigration of the soul." In addition, it is also known as "samsara." Hinduism gives all acknowledgement to the Vedas (Vedic faith) for the concept that karma, samsara, and moksha go hand-in-hand and are not separable, since this faith plays a major role in explaining as well as connecting these concepts. Reincarnation explains the Hindu belief that one's immortal soul is believed to be reborn continuously.

Even though many Hindus may disagree about the different philosophies of Hinduism, most of them seem to agree on the two fundamental beliefs of reincarnation and karma. Hinduism teaches there are two types of souls, namely, the individual soul and the universal soul. The individual soul is referred to as the "atman," which happens to be eternal and also uncreated. The universal soul is referred to as the "Brahman."

Hinduism teaches that Hindus must learn to unite the individual soul with the universal soul. By doing so, they fulfill the goal of becoming one with the ultimate reality. The Hindu scriptures tell us that the Brahman is this ultimate reality. The ultimate goal of all Hindus is to be able to break free from the wheel of misfortune (samsara); they are able to do so only by being able to unite with their universal soul.

Reincarnation refers to the ever-revolving "wheel of fortune," that is, it includes the wheel of events encompassing life, death, and rebirth. Thus what we are reaping in the current or present lifetime has everything to do with the consequences of deeds that we committed during previous lifetimes. According to the reincarnation theory, it is believed that humans can be born again either as humans, animals, insects, plants, or inanimate objects such as rocks.

What determines this kind of birth? Indeed, it is the individual's karma that determines the type of body (human, animal, insect, or plant) into which that person will be incarnated in the next lifetime; the individual's good and bad deeds that will determine the type of form in which he or she will come back in the next life cycle. For example, if someone lives a bad life and does not measure up to the standards that are expected of him, then he will come back as a lower form such as an animal, insect, or plant.

When an individual dies, the physical body is of no use and serves no purpose. But the soul lives on (it will be reborn) since it is believed to be immortal. Why should a soul go on from one birth to another? The Hindu scriptures give the following explanation:

> When the soul commits physical sins, then it goes on to be reborn as some plant form. When one sins through speech, then one goes on to be reborn as an animal or bird. Furthermore, when one sins by way of their thoughts, a human is degraded. The sins of the last and present births express bad temperament and an individual then goes on to be reborn as ugly monstrous forms.
> —Pustak Mahal, 2007

According to principles related in science, energy cannot be destroyed; it only changes form. Many times the changed form is not always visible. This same kind of thinking is applied when relating to beliefs involving reincarnation. The Bhagavad-Gita (2:22) states, "Just as a man discards his old clothes and takes on new ones, in the same way the soul discards the old body and enters a new one." A soul cannot be destroyed by any weapon or by fire, water, or air. The soul cannot die. Thus, by definition, it is considered to be eternal, omnipresent, immovable, constant, and everlasting. Just as every action has a reaction, every life has a relife.

Moksha

Hinduism offers at least three paths that an individual can choose in order to attain enlightenment. These three paths include karma marga, jnana marga, and bhakti marga. Marga means *way*. Karma marga deals with the way of action and ritual. Jnana marga deals with the way of knowledge and meditation. And bhakti marga deals with the way of devotion. Upon examining these paths an individual can easily detect that each of these paths puts a heavy emphasis on works. This is about an individual's own effort and does not allow for the application of any grace.

The process whereby a human reaches the same plane as God is dependent on works in terms of the Hindu religion, whereas God is reaching us through His grace in terms of the Christian religion. The Bible confirms this when it says, "For by grace are ye saved through faith; and that not of yourselves: it is the gift of God: Not of works, lest any man should boast" (Eph.2:8–9). God, through His grace, gives us the opportunity to have an everlasting relationship with Him, and we don't even have to do anything to earn it with our works, as it is a gift that is freely given.

Every Hindu's ultimate goal is to reach a level of attainment that releases him from the wheel of samsara, that is, the wheel of life, death, and rebirth. An individual needs to come to a realization that the self is nothing more than an illusion and only oneness or unity with a Brahman is considered to be real. With this in mind, an individual must learn to detach himself from any egotistical desires and thus strive to attain enlightenment.

Moksha means *liberation*. Sometimes it is also referred to as redemption or freedom. Just how does an individual achieve salvation or release? To achieve salvation, an individual needs to seek a release from samsara, the vicious cycle of the wheel of misfortune. "According to the concept of samsara, the stream of reality possesses the souls of those who are constantly dying and being reborn. Therefore, the goal of Hinduism is to escape this cyclical process" (Eternal Ministries, 2006).

The ultimate goal of Hinduism is to attain a release from the wheel of misfortune, that is, freedom from reincarnation (samsara), and this can be achieved only when an individual can unite with the Brahman who is considered to be the universal reality. In order for this to happen, the good karma has to outweigh the bad karma. How do we make sure this happens? How do we make sure that we possess good karma? We do this by following or choosing one of the three (or more) ways, or margas.

CHAPTER 11

SALVATION

IN ACCORDANCE WITH the teachings of Hinduism, salvation does not always come immediately and may take millions of lifetimes to attain. Furthermore, Hinduism does not teach the reality of sin or the existence of evil. Thus an individual's salvation is, for the most part, dependent upon his or her ability to nullify any bad karma. Karma functions in accordance with the law of cause and effect.

Also, in keeping with these teachings, an individual must reach the level of enlightenment or self-realization in order to attain salvation. In addition, an individual must deny reality and accept a spiritual perspective that is defined strictly by Hinduism. The concept known as "Maya," which means *illusion*, is considered to be a non-reality. It includes the physical or material world. Conversely, true reality is the belief that all is God. To go beyond Maya, an individual must transcend into the ultimate reality, or Brahman.

In accordance with the teachings of Hinduism, the attainment of salvation cannot be separated from a fundamental belief in karma and reincarnation. The concept of salvation is inseparable from that of karma, and there appears to be a direct correlation in meaning between these two terms. To attain salvation, individuals must put forth effort to improve their karma. They succeed in doing this by getting rid of their bad karma.

Once an individual gets rid of their bad karma, they may then move on to attain a higher form of existence. Furthermore, once an individual reaches this higher form of existence, then salvation becomes a state of existence whereby they do not experience samsara, that is, the constant rebirth in time and space.

—Eternal Ministries, 2000

Hindus recognize that there are at least three possible paths to salvation. These three paths are: karma yoga, which is the way of works; jnana yoga, which is the way of knowledge; and bhakti yoga, which is the way of devotion. But the Bhagavad-Gita declares that there are four margas (ways), and that each one of these margas is equally valid and beneficial. The fourth way is called the hatha yoga, and it focuses primarily on an individual's ability to maintain mental concentration.

Before discussing the three primary margas of salvation, it is important to explain the four goals of life that are permissible to Hindus. Well-known Christian author, Rick Rood, states, "Hinduism recognizes that in the course of many lifetimes people may legitimately give themselves to any of these goals." He explains the four goals as follows:

1. The first is the goal of pleasure or enjoyment, particularly through love and sexual desire. This is called kama.
2. The second legitimate aim in life is for wealth and success. This is called artha.
3. The third aim in life is moral duty or, dharma. One who gives himself to dharma renounces personal pleasure and power, to seek the common good.
4. The final aim in life is moksha—liberation from the cycle of lives in this material world, and entrance into Nirvana.

Karma Marga—The Way of Action and Ritual

This path to salvation focuses on daily duty. The best way to accumulate good karma is for individuals to fulfill both their religious and social obligations. The main focus of their religious activity is geared towards worshipping gods and goddesses, and the main focus of social obligation centers around the caste system. In terms of the religious side, a devoted Hindu must worship gods and goddesses by participating in the ceremonies that take place not only at home but also in Hindu temples.

Usually the Brahmin priests oversee all religious worship and ceremonies. The individuals who pay for these services are doing so in order to build good karma. Most of these temples are dedicated to a single god or goddess and the deities take the form of an idol or an image. In these temples, a Brahmin priest's job is multifaceted; the priest tries to wake up the god by chanting some mantras in Sanskrit, gives the god a bath (usually by milk), offers fresh flowers, offers food, and finally burns some incense. Families also perform the same services at home.

The father, or head of household, is usually the individual who leads the family in these religious ceremonies or practices. But in the absence of a father figure, the mother or older children assume this position. An individual builds up good karma by practicing these religious and spiritual rituals or ceremonies on a daily basis.

In terms of social obligations, devoted Hindus must do whatever is necessary in order to stay within their caste (at the time of their birth). In other words, an individual should stay in his or her own caste in regards to all areas of life, including the areas involving work, eating, marriage, and raising children who can carry on the tradition.

A verse from the Bhagavad-Gita (6:1) states, "One who performs the prescribed duty without seeking its fruit (for personal enjoyment) is a renunciant (sanyaasi) and a Karma yogi." In karma marga, a devotee is known to perform a lifetime of daily work and this work is dedicated to the ultimate reality. Brahma is referred to as this ultimate reality.

In order to attain self-realization, an individual does not always have to isolate himself and go to a forest or sit in a cave to perform meditations. Self-realization can also be attained through work or action. Despite any interferences or disturbances, an individual must learn to perform his duties consistently and persistently. There is no room for this individual to complain and murmur.

According to the Bhagavad-Gita, an individual has a right to work only but does not have a right to expect any fruits of his labor (actions) (Gita. 2.47). Lord Krishna mentions the following about detachment: individuals must do their duty without any attachment and must maintain an even mind whether the end result culminates in a success or failure (Gita. 18.6). People are not to worry about the end result; rather, they should perform their duty to the best of their abilities and then just walk away. Whatever comes their way, they ought to appreciate.

In the Gita, people are told that they can accomplish their duties in such a fashion by controlling their senses (Ch. 2:64–65) and desires (Ch. 2:71). Learning to control individuals' senses and desires is crucial, and their success or failure in doing so plays a key role in their ability to fulfill their obligations or duties.

Hindu author, Mr. Jayaram, stated in his article *Principles and Practice of Karma Yoga* that the karma yoga is based on the following principles:

1. Man cannot escape from performing actions, howsoever he may live. Therefore, man should not renounce actions.
2. True renunciation means *renunciation of the desire for the fruit of one's action, not the action itself.*
3. 3. The deluded man thinks egoistically that "I am the doer," not realizing that it is nature that engages men in actins through the triple gunas of sattva (purity), rajas (passion), and tamas (crudeness).
4. Actions that are performed out of desire for the fruit of action and with a sense of doership bind men to the mortal world.
5. In performing actions, one should follow the example of God who engages himself in actions, though there is nothing for him to do or achieve in the entire world.

Mr. Jayaram further adds that a true and genuine devotee must cultivate the following qualities or virtues in order to become perfect in karma yoga: detachment, equanimity of the mind, surrender to God, egolessness, single-minded devotion to God, and elimination or control of desires, especially the desire for the fruit of one's actions. Furthermore, three points are central to the karma marga: 1) one is to do his duties sincerely, 2) one is not to attach self to anything, 3) one is not to expect anything in return.

Jnana Marga—The Way of Knowledge

"Jnana" means *knowledge* and "marga" means *way*. Swami Krishnananda explains that,

> you are not the world that is seen and the world which is seen is not yourself. Such being the case, how would you bring together in a state of harmony the seer and the seen? Who is to work out this mystery? This deep analytical process, which will stun the mind of any person and debar anyone from even approaching it, this wonderful self-identical means of knowing Brahman, is called jnana, which cannot be translated into the English language easily. People say jnana means knowledge, wisdom, but they are all inadequate expressions of the operation that is taking place when Brahman is known. (Krishnananda Swamy, 2009, an on-line article).

This path heavily relies on the intellect. The greatest hindrance an individual can have to moksha (liberation) is not having sufficient knowledge concerning the true reality of the soul. Therefore, individuals should learn to discipline their moral as well as intellectual nature, and this can be accomplished by relinquishing any selfish motives and desires that they might have.

Those who choose this path must educate themselves by studying the Upanishads. In addition, an individual must also recognize deep meditation. One author states that "salvation is achieved through attaining a state of consciousness in which we realize our identity with Brahman. This is achieved through deep meditation, often as a part of the discipline of yoga" (Rood, Probe Ministries, 1994).

Those individuals who choose this path try to acquire true knowledge and thus learn to control their minds, senses, and desires. Of the three or more paths that an individual takes to achieve liberation, this path is most suitable for those individuals who are deeply intellectual. The second chapter of Bhagavad-Gita is referred to as jnana yoga and consists of the following practices:

1. Developing correct awareness of the mind, the body, and the atman, or self.
2. Purification of the body and the mind through self-discipline (atma-samyamyoga).
3. Acquiring true awareness of the world around and the supreme-self beyond: Knowledge of Sat (Truth) and Asat (Falsehood).
4. Practicing various disciplines and other techniques as a means to self-purification and elevation and elimination of thought process.

Those individuals who choose to believe in this path are convinced that it is ignorant to believe that we are individual selves and that we are not one with the Brahman (the ultimate reality). This kind of ignorance lends itself to bad action, which in turn leads to bad karma.

Bhakti Marga—The Way of Devotion

Of the three or more paths that lead to liberation (salvation), bhakti marga is considered to be the one that is superior to all of the other paths. It is also considered as being the most popular way to find God. The second most popular path is the karma marga. This path, though it can assist anyone who is sincere, is geared towards those individuals who are emotional. The Bhagavad-Gita (12:8–9) declares that a single-minded devotion to Vasudeva promises an individual a sure path to self-realization. Bhakti yoga seems to focus or dwell on selfless love.

Through ritual and devotion to a chosen deity (god or goddess), a person becomes one with the lord (as in Lord Krishna), and it is through Krishna that a person becomes one with the Brahman, who is the ultimate reality. A verse from chapter 18 of the Bhagavad-Gita states that "Abandoning all (other) duties, come to Me as thy sole refuge; from all evils I shall rescue thee: be not grieved." It is believed that an uncompromising and dedicated love towards Lord Krishna will open the way for entrance into Brahman and thus insure moksha.

CHAPTER 12

HINDU SACRED TEXTS

ALL HINDU RELIGIOUS texts or literature can be categorized into two main groups, namely, Shruti and Smriti. Shruti contains revealed truth, that is, what has been heard. Smriti contains realized truth, or what has been remembered. Shruti is similar in nature to that of statute law. It is derived from both revelation and unquestionable truth. Furthermore, this literature is considered to be eternal in terms of its utility.

Conversely, Smriti is considered to be literature that is based upon events that have occurred in the past. This type of literature has a tendency to change over time since by its very nature it is based on remembrance. Thus, it can be authoritative only to the extent that it lines up to the principles stated by Shruti.

Shruti consists of the following texts: 1) the Vedas, 2) the Upanishads, 3) the Brahmanas, and 4) the Brahma Sutras (also known as the Vedanta Sutras). The Smriti consists of the following texts: 1) the Puranas, 2) the Dharma Shastras, 3) the Ramayana (one of the great epics), 4) the Mahabharata (the other great epic), 5) the Bhagavad-Gita (considered to be the most famous and preferred of the Smriti texts), and 6) the Tantras. Due to its importance and popularity, I will mention or explain only certain sacred texts. The approximate time frames for the Shruti and Smriti texts are provided here:

Time Frame for the Shruti Texts

1. The Vedas were written around 1500–1000 B.C.
2. The Upanishads were written around 800–500 B.C.
3. The Brahmanas were written around 900–500 B.C.
4. The Brahma Sutras were written around AD100

Time Frame for the Smriti Texts

1. The Puranas were written around A.D. 400–1000
2. The Dharma Shastras were written around 100 B.C.–A.D. 200
3. The Ramayana was written around 500 B.C.
4. The Mahabharata was written around A.D. 400–300
5. The Tantras were written around A.D. 300–1100

The Vedas

In the Sanskrit language, Veda means *knowledge* or *wisdom*. A collection of hymns, prayers, chants, mantras, and ritual texts make up the Vedas. This collection is considered to contain the oldest and most authoritative texts in Hinduism. The exact date of this collection is not known for sure, but most scholars believe the date to be around 1500 B.C. Sanskrit is believed to be the official language of the Vedas and of the gods. The authors are unknown, but according to most scholars the credit most likely goes to the Brahmin priests.

The Vedas are considered to be personal, as well as eternal. The Vedic texts have been passed down from generation to generation by the Brahmin priests, both from memory and also by rote. These texts are divided into four groups: 1) the Rig Veda, 2) the Yajur Veda, 3) the Sama Veda, and 4) the Atharva Veda. Each of these four Vedas contains the following subdivisions: 1) the Aranyakas, 2) the Brahmanas, 3) the Samhitas, and 4) the Upanishads. The Vedas are said to be classified into two parts or portions, namely, the work part and the knowledge part. The work part involves rituals and the knowledge part deals with philosophy. The Upanishads (also referred to as Vedanta) belongs to the knowledge part of the Vedas.

The Rig Veda

The Rig Veda is considered to be the oldest of all the Hindu sacred texts. It contains verses of praise to the Vedic gods. One may ask, who are these Vedic gods? Here is a list of the most important Vedic gods and goddesses: Indra, Agni, Rudra, Varuna, Mitra, Ashvins, Aditi, Saraswati, Usha, and Savitar. The Vedas are divided into 10 books (also known as Mandalas) that contain approximately 1028 hymns.

All of these hymns are directed towards praising various Vedic deities. About one-fourth of these hymns are geared towards Indra, with Agni coming to a close second. Indra is in charge of the heaven (over other minor gods and sages) and is known as the slayer of the demon Vritra. Agni is the god of fire and is also seen as a messenger between humans and gods. The Rig Veda also contains the well-known, well-respected, and the famous Gayatri Mantra.

The Yajur Veda

The Yajur Veda is a handbook for the priests and it gives the instruction on how to perform the rituals and ceremonies, such as yajnas. Yajna means *sacrifice*.

The Sama Veda

The Sama Veda consists of sacred chants and melodies to be sung during worship as well as during the performance of yajnas. The classical music in India appears to borrow its roots of origin from this Veda.

The Atharva Veda

The Atharva Veda contains hymns, mantras, and incantations. This Veda mostly deals with ethical issues. In addition, it also deals with some branches of science as in Ayurveda, which happens to be the study of health and longevity.

Of the four Vedas, the Aranyakas are considered to be the forest books, which are used mainly by the hermits and saints. The Brahmanas are written in a prose style and contain the manuals of ritual and prayer for the priests. The Samhitas are the collection of hymns and mantras. Finally, the Upanishads (also referred to as Vedanta) are the books of philosophy. The Upanishads are looked up to as the end, or the conclusion, of the Vedas.

The Upanishads

The literal meaning of Upanishad means *sitting near* or *near-below-sit*. A disciple always sits next to the feet of his guru, or master, otherwise known as sitting at the master's feet. This act was done by the disciple to show respect and reverence for the master while maintaining a humble attitude.

There are at least 108 Upanishads, of which about ten or eleven are considered to be the most important. These texts were written in prose style. The Indian philosophy is primarily based on the Upanishads. In addition to philosophy, the Upanishads also provide information on: the atman (the self), Brahman (the ultimate reality), morality, and eternal life. This text also deals with such issues relating to the soul, reincarnation, karma, and moksha. Finally, the inner meditation takes precedence over any outward performance.

The Brahma Sutras

The Brahma Sutras are also referred to as "Vedanta Sutras." They were composed by the great sage Ved Vyasa, also known as the Badarayana. The author of the great epic Mahabharatha and Bhagavad-Gita is Sage Vyasa. Some individuals believe that the Vyasa could be the avatar (incarnation) of Vishnu. The Vyasa is also believed to be one of the eight immortals who have no death. Lord Hanuman (the monkey god) is also one of these eight. The sacred text tells us that immediately after birth, the Vyasa became an adult and adopted the lifestyle of an ascetic.

The Brahma Sutras are composed of four chapters (known as Adhyaya). The names of these four chapters include: 1) Avirodha (meaning non-conflict), 2) Phala (meaning fruit), 3) Sadhana (meaning practice), and 4) Samanvaya (meaning, establishing harmony). Divided among the four chapters are about 550 sayings or proverbs. Several authors have written lengthy commentaries on these Sutras.

One such author, Sri Adi Sankara, is well-known and highly respected; he abstracted a great deal of intellectual insights from each Sutra. It has been stated that "because people were less philosophically inclined in Kali-Yuga, the Upanishads and Vedanta Sutra are considered difficult to understand without the guidance of the supplementary 'smriti' literature" (Iskcon, 2009).

The Puranas

The literal meaning of Purana is *ancient* or *very old*. However, they are not really that old, as they were written right around A.D. 400 to 1000. The Puranas discusses the Trimurti (tri meaning *three* and murti meaning *gods*). These are the three gods known as the Brahma, Vishnu, and Shiva.

There are many Puranas (some written recently), but only eighteen are considered noteworthy. These eighteen texts are divided into three sets of six books. Each of these three sets is connected to one of the Trimurti—Brahma, Vishnu, and Shiva. It is believed that some Hindus consider the Puranas to be the fifth Veda.

The Puranas deal with the creation of the universe, its destruction, and renovation, the genealogy of the gods and the patriarchs, the reigns of ancient rulers, rules for living, descriptions of various worlds and, lastly, many of the popular myths and stories. It has been said that the stories and tales of the Puranas form "an integral part of the very fabric of Hindu culture" (Iskcon, 2009).

The two most popular of the Puranas are the "Bhagavad-Gita" and the "Bhagavat Purana," also referred to as "Srimad Bhagavatam."

Bhagavatam texts consist of more than 18,000 verses and are divided into twelve volumes. The main focus is on Lord Vishnu and his ten avatars, especially that of the 8th avatar, Lord Krishna.

The Dharma Shastras

To find the law codes of Hinduism, people can look to the Dharma Shastras. This text mainly focuses on three topics or subjects: 1) civil and criminal law, 2) codes of conduct, and 3) punishment and atonement. This text introduces the Laws of Manu. Manu was the ruler of mankind but also was the first lawgiver.

It is believed that the word "man" came from "Manu." There were others who wrote the Brahma Shastras, and one of those authors happens to be the great Sage Narada who is both liked and very well respected. Narada is one of the created sons of the triune god Brahma.

The Bhagavad-Gita

"Bhagavan" means *god* and "gita" means *song* and, thus, is referred to as "the Song of God" or "Lord's Song." The Gita is part of the great epic Mahabharata. It consists of eighteen chapters and about 700 verses. The Gita is not only considered to be one of the most sacred but also one of the most popular scriptures of Hinduism. In addition, it is also the best known and possibly most widely read book.

It is very likely that many Hindus (maybe even most) possess or own a copy of the Gita so that anyone in the family can read it at a moment's notice. Lord Krishna is the main character, and he is none other than Lord Vishnu in his eighth avatar (incarnation). This could be the main reason why many Hindus consider the Gita to be a direct message of Vishnu.

Both the Gita and the epic Mahabharata were written by the great sage Ved Vyasa, also known as Badarayana. Some folks strongly believe that Ved Vyasa is also one of the incarnations of Vishnu. The Gita is all about an intense dialogue between Krishna and Arjuna (his closest and favorite devotee), which takes place right in the middle of the battlefield of Kurukshetra (probably the modern-day state of Rajasthan).

Kurukshetra is the place where the battle of Mahabharata took place. The battle took place between the five sons of King Pandu and the 100 sons of blind Dhritarashtra. These two kings were brothers, thus making their sons (105 in total) cousins. The five sons of Pandu won the battle after about eighteen days of fighting, as the general belief in these epics seems to suggest that good always triumphs over bad or evil.

The Gita provides instructions on how to conduct our lives on a daily basis and strongly urges that an individual does so by keeping God at the center of everything that they say and do. On a more personal level, the message that I received in the past each time I read the Gita was as follows: 1) to do my duty without any compromise. 2) After doing my duty, I am not to expect anything in return. If nothing happens, then I would not be disappointed. If something were to come my way, then I must be appreciative. 3) I must learn to exercise detachment from any and all materialistic pleasures; and, lastly, 4) I must accept the fact that it is God who is in charge, and since he controls everything, I play a very small role in the outcome.

My parents once told me that if an individual were to read the Gita on a regular basis and maintain the necessary faith, that person could expect to be blessed in almost all areas of life—spiritually, physically, mentally, materialistically, career wise, as well as in marriage. There was a time in my life when I placed the Gita right next to my pillow each night when I went to bed.

Some folks believe that the Gita is just as relevant today as it was centuries ago and can be taken at face value. Figuratively speaking, the Gita is considered to be the New Testament of Hinduism. The message of Krishna is considered to be the "Gospel of Krishna."

In the Gita, "Krishna tells a young warrior, Arjuna, that though death and killing are unpleasant, both life and death are minor compared with eternal values. Krishna gradually reveals himself to Arjuna as the Supreme Lord, and he teaches Arjuna to depend on him for liberation (moksha)" (Braswell, 1994). The Gita is not only very popular in India but it also seems to be very popular in the United States as well as in Europe.

The man responsible for starting the International Society for Krishna Consciousness (ISKCON) in New York in 1966 was the late A.C. Bhakti Vedanta Swami Prabhupada, also known as Srila Prabhupada. In the Gita, Krishna said, "give me your mind and give me your heart, give me your offerings and your adoration" (Gita 9:34). The Gita ends with Prince Arjuna being completely devoted to Krishna (Vishnu). He is ready and willing to kill his relatives in battle by convincing himself that he is only doing his duty as per Krishna.

CHAPTER 13

THREE MAIN GODS

The Trimurti

TRIMURTI IS REFERRED to as the "holy trinity." It consists of three godheads, Brahma, Vishnu, and Shiva. Brahma is known as the creator; Vishnu is known as the preserver; and Shiva is known as the destroyer. These godheads also have many other names. But in accordance with the famous saying, "Behind all successful men there is a woman," the same kind of thinking can also be applied to the Trimurti.

Brahma's wife is Saraswati, Vishnu's wife is Lakshmi, and Shiva's wife is Parvati. All of these wives play a major role in assisting with the duties of their husbands, especially in terms of keeping and maintaining a balance between humans, demigods, and demon kings. Regardless of how famous these gods might be, an individual cannot find any reference to the trinity in the Vedas. As a matter of fact, in the Vedic period, Vishnu was a minor solar god and Shiva was almost non-existent. Where do each of the trinity live? Brahma lives and rules the Brahmalok, Vishnu lives and rules the Vaikunth, and Shiva is the ruler of Kailash (probably the modern-day Himalayan mountains).

Brahma

Brahma is the first god of the Trimurti. He is credited with the creation of all living things as well as the universe. According to history, no one created him since he created himself. Brahma goes by many names, but the one name that stands out among the others is "Prajapati." Praja means *people* and pati means *lord*. Thus he is known as "lord of the people." Some folks believe that Brahma was born in a lotus flower that came from the navel of Vishnu. There are others who believe that he was born in a golden egg that came out of the waters. The priestly caste, the Brahmin, is believed to have been derived from Brahma.

Brahma has four heads and four hands. According to history, he used to have five heads. Lord Shiva cut off one of his heads in anger because of something Brahma had done; he either lied or misrepresented himself. As for the four heads or faces, there have been different interpretations of them such as: 1) four heads represent four directions, 2) four heads represent four Vedas, 3) four heads represent four castes, 4) the four heads represent the four Yugas. There are four Yugas: Satya Yuga, Treta Yuga, Dwapara Yuga, and Kali Yuga. Hindus believe that this current generation is living in the Kali Yuga, meaning that time is short or the end is near.

Brahma is not considered to be a popular god. In fact, there few temples that have been built for Brahma. There are many more temples that have been built for Vishnu and Shiva. There may only be two temples in all of India that have been built exclusively for Brahma—the temple of Pushkar near Ajmer and the temple of Khed near Idar. But one can find Brahma placed as an attendant god in almost all the temples allocated to Vishnu and Shiva.

Vishnu

The literal meaning of Vishnu is *the giver and provider* of things. Vishnu is considered to be the most popular god in India. In comparison to the role that either Brahma or Shiva play, Vishnu plays a much more vital role. On the one hand, Brahma's role was just about finished after he created the universe. Conversely, Shiva is almost always engaged in deep meditation, and he is waiting for the day when he is supposed to destroy the universe.

Of course there were times when Brahma and Shiva had to appear to a sage or a king or a demon king in order to grant a boon or wish. However, for the most part, they remain unengaged. An individual can easily understand how busy Vishnu must be since he is expected to be in charge of both heaven and earth.

Vishnu makes Vaikunth his residence. He rests or sleeps on a big serpent named Adisesha. His wife, Lakshmi, also sits on the serpent at his feet and attends him. Vishnu's skin color is that of a dark blue cloud, and Krishna's color is the same. Vishnu has four arms, and he is usually in a standing posture. In each of his arms he holds a conch, discus, mace, and lotus. "He has been compared to the Christian concept of God" (Braswell, 1994). Vishnu is the god of grace and love, and he has been compared to Jesus.

One of Vishnu's many roles is to maintain law and order in the universe. His job is to restore moral order. When things go out of order, Vishnu comes down to earth to take care of his business. Some folks believe that, all in all, there are about twenty-three incarnations (avatars) of Vishnu, but only ten have been generally accepted, of which nine have already taken place and the 10th one is yet to take place in the future.

The ten incarnations of Vishnu that are generally accepted include: 1) the Fish incarnation (Matsyavatara), 2) the Tortoise incarnation (Kurmavatara), 3) the Boar incarnation (Varahavatara), 4) the Man-Lion incarnation (Narasimhavatara), 5) the Dwarf incarnation (Vamanavatara), 6) the incarnation of Parasurama (Parasuramavatara, also known as Rama with an axe), 7) the incarnation of Rama (Ramavatara), 8) the incarnation of Krishna (Krishnavatara), 9) the incarnation of Buddha (Budhavatara), and 10) the incarnation of Kalki (this is the avatar that is yet to come in the future). The two most popular avatars are the Rama and Krishna.

In the Bhagavad-Gita, Lord Krishna told Arjuna, "whenever there is a decline of righteousness and rise of unrighteousness, then I send forth Myself. For the protection of the good, for the destruction of the wicked, and for the establishment of righteousness, I come into being from age to age" (Pollock, 2002).

Shiva

It is not easy to describe Lord Shiva because on one hand he is part of the trinity and on the other, as Lord Maheshwara, he is known to represent the trinity all by himself. The different aspects of his character portray him as being the creator, the preserver, and the destroyer. Shiva is the second most popular god, right behind Vishnu. His physical appearance is not that appealing; he looks a little odd or different.

Shiva sits on a tiger skin, semi-naked, and has at least one snake wrapped around each of his arms and his neck. His body is covered with ashes. Shiva has many names, of which Nataraja is one of the popular ones. Nata means *dance* and raja means *king*, and thus he is master of all dance forms.

Shiva is being worshipped either in the form of a statute (as a human form) or in a lingam form. A linga (a mark of Shiva) is an egg-shaped stone representing Shiva. Some statutes show both the male and female side of Shiva. Shiva's right side represents the male part, whereas Shiva's left side represents the female part. This is a way of acknowledging that gods and goddesses are equal and that male and female are also equal. In other words, Shiva possesses both masculine and feminine qualities and characteristics. Besides being the god of destruction, he is also the god of transformation and regeneration.

As part of the Trimurti, Shiva's role may appear to be limited; he is waiting for the end of time in order to bring about destruction. But when separated from the Trimurti he is a god with many faces, many names, and many attributes. He is portrayed as a loving husband, a dedicated and nurturing father, and an astute yogi. When he wants to display and demonstrate anger, he represents himself as Rudra, who is feared by all.

He is the lord of kailash, also known as the modern-day Himalayan mountain range, the place where he lives and rules. He is known as Umapathi, being the husband of Uma, the mother goddess. He is known to take on many names and forms in order to protect his devotees. His devotees include humans, demigods, and demon kings, as in Ravanasura (or Lankeshwara), the villain of the great epic Ramayana.

CHAPTER 14

THE CONSORTS

SHIVA IS MARRIED to Parvati and they have two sons, Kumara Swami (he goes by other names as well) and Ganesha. Shiva has a third eye that is affixed between his two eyes in the center of his forehead. He usually keeps his third eye closed. But, if he chooses to open his third eye, beware, since everything that is in front of that eye will be burned to ashes. Shiva's main weapon is a trident, which looks like a huge fork. His trident has three tines of which each represents creation, protection, and destruction of the universe. Shiva's vehicle of choice is the Bull Nandi.

Unlike Vishnu, Shiva did not incarnate himself. He has many manifestations, and many goddesses seem to be associated with him. Shakti and Kali are two well-known and feared goddesses. The goddess Shakti "represents female power and fertility to complement the male Shiva. Kali, the great goddess and Shiva's consort, represents violent power. Kali is greatly feared and sexual orgies have been connected to her cult of worship" (Braswell, 1994). Conversely, the goddess Parvati (another consort of Shiva) represents good fortune and prosperity. Between Shiva and his consorts, an individual can find both positive and negative characteristics.

Saraswati

Saraswati is the wife of Brahma. She is the goddess of knowledge, learning, and the arts. She holds the status of being recognized as the first goddess to have been worshipped. The literal meaning of Saraswati means *the one who flows*. She happens to be the favorite goddess of many students since she is the goddess that represents knowledge and education. As a teenager, I remember praying to her each time I had to take an exam.

The Veena is Saraswati's favorite musical instrument. Her favorite books are the Vedas, and her vehicle of choice is either a beautiful white swan or a peacock. She is personified by grace and elegance and is usually seated on a lotus. She has four hands and holds a book, lotus, rosary, and Veena in each of her four hands.

Lakshmi

Lakshmi is the wife of Vishnu. She is the goddess of wealth and happiness and is known to bring about good luck. But an individual should not be worshipping and praying to her just for the sake of gaining wealth. With that kind of motive, she may not answer the prayer. Thus she prefers to see some personal responsibility from each devotee as well. An individual is likely to find either a framed picture of goddess Lakshmi or some other kind of picture of her, such as is often found depicted on a calendar or displayed in many businesses.

The business owners hang her picture in their businesses, hoping and believing that she will bring a lot of wealth to their business. The goddess Lakshmi also has four hands and is sometimes seen sitting on a lotus flower. She holds one lotus flower in two hands, an Aum symbol in one hand, and gifts of prosperity in the other hand. This goddess is usually seated at the feet of Vishnu and is often seen massaging his feet. Her preference for choice of vehicles is the great owl.

The goddess Lakshmi has many aspects that are connected to various forms of wealth. There are eight forms of Lakshmi known as Ashtalakshmis. The word Ashta means *number eight*.

Each one of the eight forms deals with a particular type of wealth. The eight Lakshmis are as follows: 1) Adi Lakshmi (First), 2) Dhairya Lakshmi (Courage), 3) Dhana Lakshmi (Riches), 4) Dhanya Lakshmi (Crops), 5) Gaja Lakshmi (Elephants), 6) Santana Lakshmi (Children), 7) Vidya Lakshmi (Education), and 8) Vijaya Lakshmi (Victory).

The goddess Lakshmi also incarnates herself each time her husband, Vishnu, incarnates into a human form. She does this in order to bring about law and order, balance, or, specifically, to restore "Dharma." Some of her incarnations include Padma, Dharani, Sita, and Rukmini. Padma was the wife of Vamana, Dharani was the wife of Parasu Rama, Sita was the wife of Rama, and Rukmini was the wife of Krishna. Vamana, Parasu Rama (Rama with an axe), Rama, and Krishna are all incarnations of Vishnu.

Parvati

Parvati is the wife of lord Shiva, and the daughter of the mountain king named Parvatha. Devotees of Parvati worship and revere her by many names. She is worshipped not only as the wife of Shiva, but also as the mother goddess. Some of the other names that she goes by include Uma, Haimavathi, Dakshayani, and Shakti. Of course, there are many other names and forms of this goddess.

Of all the names and forms that Parvati takes on, the most popular ones include Annapurna and Gayatri. Annapurna represents food and the source of all food. She is also known by the name Gayatri, the main deity of the Gayatri Mantra. Some folks believe that those who read Gayatri Mantra on a regular basis will be blessed in many ways.

Parvati's name as the mother goddess is Durga. One of the Puranas, Devi Bhagavatham, is believed to be devoted to the goddess Parvati. According to this story, the goddess Durga slew a powerful demon named Mahishasura. This demon is capable of creating havoc both in the heavens and on earth. Out of fear and desperation, the sages as well as the gods approached goddess Durga and requested that she take care of this demon once and for all.

Mahishasura is a bull-headed demon with a lot of powers. This demon's powers were probably given to him by Brahma, a god who can be easily pleased. Once the trinity gods give their word, it must be upheld. Any changes to that effect have to be worked in accordance with the word of these gods. This demon is creating a lot of trouble both in the heavens as well as on earth.

This troublemaking has resulted in all of the gods and humans being stressed out. But not a single god was able to fight him. So all the gods pleaded with the goddess Durga to handle him and she agreed to do the job. During her encounter with the demon, she approached him riding on a lion (some texts say tiger). She had several hands in which she held a powerful weapon. She fought and defeated the demon, thus putting an end to his deeds.

The goddess Durga (Parvati) also slew several other demons. Because of what she did to all these demons, she earned so much respect that some folks even consider her to rank above the Trimurti in terms of importance. Furthermore, she earned the reputation to fight against and eventually destroy evil.

One Hindu author describes goddess Durga as follows:

> Durga as the controller of the universe and the Highest Self has a trinity of her own represented by 'Maha Saraswati,' 'Maha Lakshmi,' and 'Maha Kali.' These trinity parts are not considered to be counterparts to Brahma, Vishnu, and Mahesh, but as the Trinity itself, representing the creative, preservative, and destructive aspects of Durga, known as 'Ishwari' or 'Maha Devi.'
> —Jayaram, 2009

A review of all the different aspects of Durga reveals that Maha Kali is most likely considered the most fearsome. Maha Kali has ten faces and ten feet and she wears a garland of skulls (slain heads). She also holds many destructive and powerful weapons in each of her hands.

CHAPTER 15

OTHER IMPORTANT GODS

Lord Ganesha

GANESHA IS ALWAYS known as Lord Ganesha. He is the second youngest son of Shiva and Parvati. The other son is Kartikeya, and he is known by many names. In many family homes, the oldest son is called "Kumara Swami." Ganesha is one of the gods who is feared by many Indians. Some folks argue that Ganesha is the most revered (and probably most feared) of all the Hindu gods.

Before starting any religious ceremony or conducting any auspicious occasion, it is customary to offer the first prayers and respect to Ganesha. Some folks strongly believe that Ganesha is capable of removing and eliminating all debilitating obstacles that may be confronting their devotees.

When individuals put Ganesha first in their lives, they can expect to receive blessings. Those blessings can take the form of success, wealth, promotion, raises, fame, status, and prosperity. Ganesha can be easily pleased, and he does not put heavy demands on his devotees. All he expects is for them to offer him their first prayers, some chanting (of the mantras) and a little durva grass. Ganesha is considered to be the god of learning and knowledge.

Ganesha has the head of an elephant. Many stories explain how he got the head of an elephant, but one believed by most goes like this: Parvati created Ganesha from dirt and gave him life and powers. Parvati wanted to be protected while Shiva was away. One day when Shiva returned home, Ganesha did not let Shiva through, not recognizing Shiva or his powers. Shiva became very angry and cut off Ganesha's head. When Parvati started to grieve for her son, Shiva, in his compassion and love for her, killed an elephant and put its head on Ganesha.

Ganesha has a huge belly, about which there is an interesting story. Once upon a time there was a ruthless demon named Anlasur. He created havoc everywhere he went, including the heavens and on earth. He did not spare anyone, especially the gods. He would literally swallow people alive, both innocent folk as well as godly sages and saints.

Thus all the gods first approached Lord Indra, who is in charge of the heavens. Indra fought with this demon several times, but the demon defeated him each time. Then all the gods went to Shiva for help. Shiva told the gods that only Ganesha could handle this demon. Finally, as a last resort, the gods approached Ganesha for help and he agreed to confront the demon. Since Ganesha has a huge potbelly, he swallowed this demon alive.

The story goes on to relate that right after swallowing the demon, Ganesha began to have a burning sensation in his stomach. Although many remedies were tried, none were successful, which left Ganesha in great pain. A godly sage by the name of Kashyap heard about the situation and immediately rushed to Mount Kailash (where Shiva lives and rules). There he collected twenty-one stems of durva grass and offered them to Ganesha.

As soon as Ganesha ate this grass, all of his pain and burning went away. In addition to the durva grass, Ganesha was also very fond of laddoos (a sweet desert). Any offering that has no laddoos is considered to be incomplete. Lastly, besides the durva grass and laddoos, Ganesha was very fond of jaggery, also known as brown sugar.

Lord Hanuman

Hanuman is known as the monkey king or the monkey god. He is the son of Vayu and Anjana. Vayu is none other than the wind god or god of the wind. Hanuman has the head and tail of a monkey. From the neck down, he has a human body that represents masculinity and strength. Hanuman plays a key role in the great epic Ramayana and is considered to be Lord Rama's closest and most favored devotee. As mentioned before, Rama is none other than Vishnu in his seventh incarnation.

My favorite god was Hanuman, whom I worshipped and surrendered my all to during my formative years. I worshipped this god in accordance with my own free will, whereas I worshipped and prayed to Ganesha, Venkateswara, and others out of fear of condemnation.

The characteristics of Hanuman include being loyal, faithful, strong, clever, dependable, and trustworthy. There is an interesting childhood story about Hanuman. When he was about five or six years old, he was playing and became very hungry. He looked at the sun and thought that it was a fruit. Immediately he flew towards the sun so that he could pluck and eat it.

This made the god Indra very concerned. In order to protect the sun god, Indra threw his powerful weapon (vajra) at Hanuman. Immediately, Hanuman was injured and fell to the ground and broke his jaw. This injury made the god Vayu (Hanuman's father) so angry that he went to Patal. Patal is a place considered to be the underworld or hell that is believed to be located beneath the earth. With the wind god gone, the world was becoming restless because people were becoming somewhat suffocated and feeling breathless.

Out of concern, all of the gods approached Vayu and began to plead with him to show mercy. The gods immediately began to bless Hanuman. Brahma and Indra granted Hanuman several wishes or boons. The gods blessed Hanuman in such a way that no weapon of any kind would ever be able to injure or slay him. In addition, the gods also blessed him in such a way that no one would ever be able to kill him. Hanuman was given the opportunity to die by his own will and at his own time of choosing. That is why this god is sometimes referred to as Chiranjeeva, meaning *one who lives forever*.

Many Hindus believe that Shiva could have incarnated himself as Hanuman. "He is often addressed by using the prefix 'Sankatmochan'— one who liberates from crises" (Pustak Mahal, 2007). When it comes to ranking the gods in terms of their ability to practice humility, Hanuman scores the highest position. But he does not always have a good memory, especially when it relates to his strength. For example, he constantly needs someone to remind him of his strength and powers. Those who offer prayers to him usually read the Hanuman Chalisa.

Hanuman Chalisa has about forty verses and is part of the great epic Ramayana. The Hanuman Chalisa is what I read many times each day for forty consecutive days, all the time hoping and believing that by doing so I would receive protection from any obstacles or hindrances. Hanuman temples can be found all over India. Wherever there is a temple devoted to Lord Rama, an individual can find Hanuman in that temple as well.

CHAPTER 16

THE CASTE SYSTEM—
THE FOUR VARNAS

THE CONCEPT OF a different class system, in terms of social class, probably emerged during the Indo-Aryan time. These social classes were based on one's color and birth. "The pattern of social class in Hinduism is called the 'Caste System.' The basic caste is called 'varna,' or 'color.' There are subcastes, also referred to as 'Jati,' within each of the castes" (Ross, 2005). An individual's own duties and obligations are regulated by the four social classes, or Vamas, but also by the four stages of life, or Ashrams.

The four types of castes include the Brahmins, Kshatriyas, Vaishyas, and the Shudras. The four stages of life include the 1) Brahmacharya, a stage of the student; 2) Grahastya, a stage of the householder; 3) Vanaprastya, a stage of the forest dweller; and, 4) Sanyasi, a stage of the wandering ascetic.

The Hindus believe that these stages of life apply only to those who are twice born, including the Brahmins, Kshatriyas, and the Vaishyas. In order to understand the complexities of the caste system (or the social class), it is recommended that an individual read *The Laws of Manu*, which was probably written sometime around A.D. 100.

Brahmins

The Brahmin caste includes individuals from such professions as priests, scholars, teachers, counselors, intellectuals, educators, and philosophers. Individuals belonging to this caste tend to instinctively possess both educational and spiritual leadership. From the beginning of time, Brahmins took on the responsibility for preserving and safeguarding the Vedas, as well as other important sacred texts.

But more recently, as times have changed, Brahmins are entering many other fields, including, acting, politics, business, medicine, science, technology, and administration. Brahmins are primarily motivated by knowledge and tend to choose the path of jnana marga.

Kshatriya

The Kshatriyas caste includes the warriors, rulers, kings, queens, princes, princesses, executives, administrators, military, police, Maharajas, and Maharanis. Individuals belonging to this caste are usually quite wealthy. They are not motivated by power and action; rather, they tend to choose the path of karma marga, which is the way of action.

Vaishya

The Vaishyas caste includes the farmers, merchants, business people, trades people, actors, and actresses. Individuals belonging to this caste include the skilled-labor workforce. They are motivated by material objects, and they tend to choose the path of bhakti marga, which is the way of devotion.

Shudra

The Shudras caste includes individuals who are the artisans, workers, craftsmen, peasants, and slaves. This group includes the unskilled labor workforce. Since the motivations of this caste are in question, they are categorized as being unmotivated people. In addition to their motivation, their hygiene habits are also in question. Examples include (but not limited to): not brushing teeth regularly, not bathing daily, not wearing clean clothes, using foul language, and so on. They choose the path of bhakti marga, which is the way of devotion.

The ISKCON (International Society for Krishna Consciousness) has provided an excellent definition of the duties and responsibilities associated with each of the castes within the caste system. Their explanation is as follows:

Brahmins

1. Are expected to live very frugally.
2. Study and teach the Vedas.
3. Perform sacrifice and religious ceremonies.
4. Teach others how to perform religious rituals.
5. Accept alms and also give in charity.
6. Offer guidance, especially to the Kshatriyas.
7. Provide medical care and general advice, free of charge.
8. Know Brahman (spirit, the self, God).
9. Develop all ideal qualities, especially honesty, integrity, cleanliness, purity, austerity, knowledge, and wisdom.

Kshatriyas

1. Protect the citizens from harm, especially women, children, Brahmins, and the elderly.
2. Ensure that the citizens perform their prescribed duties and advance spiritually.
3. Are the first into battle and never flee the battlefield.
4. Are true to their royal word.
5. Never refuse a challenge.
6. Develop noble qualities, such as power, chivalry, and generosity.
7. Levy taxes (from the Vaishyas only).
8. Never accept charity under any circumstances.
9. Take counsel, especially from the Brahmins.
10. Know the Hindu scriptures, especially the artha-shastras.
11. Deal uncompromisingly with crime and lawlessness.

12. Take responsibility for shortcomings in their kingdom.
13. Conquer their own minds and senses to enjoy only according to scriptural injunction.
14. Beget an heir.

Vaishyas

1. Protect animals (especially the cows) and the land.
2. Create wealth and prosperity.
3. Maintain workers with abundant food and clothes.
4. Trade ethically.
5. Give taxes to the Kshatriyas (the ruling class).

Shudras

1. Render service to others.
2. Take pride in their work and be loyal.
3. Follow general moral principles (example, not to steal).
4. Marry (the only compulsory rite of passage).

A Final Note on the Caste System

The following statements, for the most part, are true, and probably more fittingly apply to earlier times. However, there are always exceptions to the rule.

The caste system embraces the concept that an individual inherits his social status from his parents at the time of his birth. Thus an individual does not have a choice in the matter concerning his assignment to a certain caste. Furthermore, individuals cannot simply move on to enter another caste. Once an assignment has been made in terms of caste at birth, an individual must remain in that caste for his entire life.

In general, members of each caste tend to socialize only with others who belong to their assigned caste. There are certain professions that seem to fit better with certain caste members. For example, priests often belong to the Brahmin caste. An individual's caste also appears to determine an individual's duties or dharma.

Furthermore, marriage between members of different castes is not entertained or encouraged.

Only the Brahmins, Kshatriyas, and Vaishyas are considered to be twice born. The term twice born should not be confused with that of reincarnation. The first birth takes place when an individual leaves his mother's womb. The second birth takes place at the time of his initiation, which is somewhat equivalent to Christianity's version of confirmation.

The Shudras do not undergo this initiation because of the underlying assumption that they are not serious enough about any spiritual discipline. Contrary to popular belief or generalization, many Shudras tend to be very spiritual in nature, not to mention the fact that a great many saints have come from the Shudra caste.

There is another caste, which appears to be an offshoot of the Shudra caste, namely, the Outcaste. These are the polluted laborers and the untouchables. These people are referred to as dalit, or the downtrodden. Individuals belonging to this caste do all menial and dirty work, which includes such activities as cleaning the streets, sewer work, and taking care of dead animal and human bodies. These individuals are almost always at your service. And they tend to choose the path of bhakti marga, which is the way of devotion.

Although the caste system was outlawed in the 1950s, many individuals still recognize and practice the associated caste system beliefs in accordance with age-old traditions and sentiments. Not only is the caste system illegal, but from a moral and spiritual standpoint, even the sacred texts are not in agreement with its beliefs. Careful observation and consideration reveals that the four Varnas or the caste system (or the social class) appears to be more of a man-made concept as opposed to anything else.

For example, the Vedas (the Rig Veda) state that "it is said that there is no difference amongst people at birth. None is big or small. All are equal. And all must be united in pursuing their goals. Any differentiation on the basis of caste is groundless. There is no religious sanctity. And any kind of untouchability between castes is a slur on humanity. God is influenced by one's actions and not by one's Caste" (Bhalla on the Rig Veda-5/60/5, 2007).

SECTION THREE

CUSTOMS, PRACTICES, RITUALS, AND WORSHIP

CHAPTER 17

CUSTOMS AND RITUALS

MANY DIFFERENT HINDU rituals are practiced, but the most important ones deal with an individual's birth, marriage, and death.

Birth

The ceremony practiced to recognize an individual's birth is referred to as the infant welcoming ritual. This ritual usually takes place right around the time when the infant is about seven months of age. According to one author, "traditionally, birth rites included a prenatal rite for the prospective father to affect the child to be fair or dark, a learned son or daughter and so on" (Pollock, 2002).

A child's first consumption of solid food is also considered to be a celebrated highlight in an individual's life, thus friends and relatives come together in large numbers for a rice-eating ceremony to recognize this important event. Right after the ceremony, the parents host a big reception for everyone in attendance. Some families go so far as to hire catering services for this event.

Marriage

In accordance with Hindu tradition, marriages are usually arranged. Lately, however, this tradition is changing somewhat. It is becoming acceptable for both parties to have to agree to all the terms and conditions set forth in the marriage agreement. Authors Brandon Toropov and Father Luke Buckles point out that "these families incorporate five ceremonies: 1) a verbal contract between the male parents or guardians of the bride and groom, 2) the giving-away of the bride by her father or guardian, 3) a welcoming ceremony for the new couple, 4) a hand-holding ritual, and 5) a walking rite."

Of the three rituals, the marriage ceremony is considered to be the most important. In general, Hindu weddings are celebrated on a grand scale and involve many activities and details that require close attention. For instance, parents must find a suitable spouse for their son or daughter. Once both parties agree on the selection of the spouse, then a Brahmin priest (as in an astrologer) has to be consulted for his advice. The priest then studies and compares each of the marriage partner's horoscopes in great detail, including such aspects as the position of the stars, zodiac signs, and other religious details at the time of each partner's birth.

If the priest finds that the two partner's horoscopes are favorable in support of marriage, then the details concerning the dowry are discussed. In accordance with Indian custom, the bride's father or family is expected to pay a dowry to the groom's father or family. The dowry usually includes such things as cash, jewelry, clothing, and sometimes a vehicle. Depending on the financial status of the bride's family, a vehicle can entail either a two-wheeler or an automobile.

Marriages take place in temples, community halls, or outdoors under big tents. The actual wedding ceremony usually takes place on a mandap (a small stage). A Brahmin priest is given control of the entire wedding ceremony. This priest arranges for the preparation of a sacred fire that is usually two feet by two feet in size. The bride and groom are told to walk around the sacred fire maybe seven times. As one author describes, The seven steps represent: 1) food,

2) strength, 3) prosperity, 4) well-being, 5) children, 6) happy seasons, and 7) harmony in their marriage" (Pollock, 2002). Both quotes are from the same author and author Pollock is referenced in the bibliography section taking the seven steps concludes the ceremony, and guests begin to get ready for the big feast that follows. A typical Hindu wedding is known to last for about three days and, in some cases, it may even last for up to five days.

Death

Hindus believe in the cremation of the body after death. This belief is related to the close ties that Hinduism has with reincarnation. The physical body, once it dies, is of no use and is of no concern. But, the soul (atman) is important since it is the soul that travels from one body to the other.

In preparation for the funeral rites, the dead body goes through several rituals such as being bathed, being wrapped in a new clean cloth, and being laid on a stretcher. Once the body is taken to the graveyard, the body is laid on a wooden pyre (a wooden bed, about three feet high). In accordance with the Hindu tradition, only a male (usually the eldest son) can set fire to the pyre.

If the family of the deceased does not have any sons, then another influential male member of the family (for example an uncle) can fulfill this obligation. There are some cases whereby either a close friend of the family or a distant relative was allowed to set fire to the pyre as long as the individual was a male. It is my understanding that females are not encouraged or expected to come to the graveyard.

CHAPTER 18

WORSHIP AND PRACTICES

WHEN HINDUS WORSHIP, they are conducting an activity known as puja. A puja can take place either at a home, in the temple, or sometimes at a community center. There are many ways to please a god, and puja is definitely one important activity that many people choose. This activity is usually performed on a daily basis. In India, almost every single home, cottage, hut, apartment, or other dwelling place has a shrine, picture frames, or calendar that presents images of gods and goddesses. Hindus are very big on performing activities such as pujas and praying.

Even though a lot of homes in India have many images or idols of gods and goddesses on display, many families tend to have a favorite deity. There is a lot of attention directed towards that particular deity. In order to perform a puja, an individual must have on hand certain items such as a fruit, some rice, a few flowers, incense, sandalwood paste, or milk, and usually a sweet (dessert) of some kind.

A lighted lamp is also used while performing a puja. Some individuals may even use candles as a substitute for a lamp. The lamp is usually held in the right hand and is waved in a clockwise circular motion at least three times. While waving the lamp or candle, an individual engages in chanting a mantra, saying a prayer, or singing a hymn and perhaps sometimes even a religious song.

Temples and Homes

Hindu temples are called mandirs. These temples are built in a range of sizes, from very large elaborate buildings that can accommodate several hundred devotees to smaller shrines of more simple design which are usually located in small villages. Some temples are built to honor either one god or goddess such as Hanuman, Shiva, or Kali. Others are built to honor only one main deity (god or goddess), but it also is built to honor other deities as well.

For example, if there is temple devoted to Lord Rama as the main deity, it will also contain a small statue of Hanuman (the monkey god). The idols in temples are usually well decorated with a garland of fresh flowers. In most cases, devotees offer expensive jewelry, not to mention large cash offerings, to the gods and goddesses.

Lord Venkateshwara (Lord V) is considered to be an avatar (incarnation of Vishnu). The temple that is devoted to Lord V is in a place called Tirupati, which is located in the state of Andhra Pradesh, the state of my birth. This temple is considered the busiest as well as the most visited place of worship in the world. Furthermore, this temple is also known to be the wealthiest in the world.

An estimated 40,000 devotees visit this temple (each day) from all the over the country. The daily offerings, including cash, gold, and silver, usually amount to about $700,000 per day. Many devotees who visit this temple have their heads shaved, regardless of sex or age. This is the same god to whom I promised that I would climb the approximate 5,000 steps up to the temple if he would help me obtain a visa to come to the United States.

Before entering any temple, worshippers must remove their shoes or sandals because each temple is considered a dwelling place for the deity. Every inch of the temple (or mandir) is considered to be holy. According to most Hindus, worshipping and praying to the statues or idols is not considered to be idolatry since Hindus strongly believe that each and every statue is inhabited by the god it represents.

Only a Brahmin priest is allowed to perform the pujas, as well as other religious or sacred ceremonies. Hindus believe that "Brahmin is the mouthpiece of Brahma" (Bhalla, 2007). Furthermore, the Brahmin caste has been recognized as being the priestly caste since the beginning of recorded time. The sacred texts describe Brahmin as the "ultimate reality."

Sacred Cows

A cow is considered to be very holy and sacred in India, thus cows are allowed to roam anywhere that they wish to go, regardless of whether they roam on city roads or the highways. When they cross the streets, they are to be given the right of way. Hindus believe that the gods reside within the body of a cow. Recognition of the cow is considered to be an essential part of most religious ceremonies. A cow is believed to have the ability to promote good health and give long life. Many sacred texts endorse the cow in a very positive and powerful manner.

One religious text declares that "the cow is a universal mother." The Vedas declare that "the cow is the mother of Rudras; she is a daughter of the Vasus; she is the sister of Surya; and she is a storehouse of ghee that is like the celestial nectar" (Bhalla, 2007). The Vedas also state that cow's milk is very beneficial and the benefits include helping to overcome debility, helping to regain lost physical (as well as mental) health, and promoting intelligence. In the Bhagavad-Gita, Krishna identifies himself with the sacred cow "Kamadhenu."

CHAPTER 19

HINDUISM VERSUS CHRISTIANITY

THERE ARE VERY few similarities between Hinduism and Christianity. Both of these religions ascribe to a belief in God and follow a written book. Followers believe in prayer, giving, and agree on certain things, such as honoring your parents and being a good role model to your children. Hinduism is also in agreement with Christianity in that all is not right with the world and with human existence in it. Also, both teach that the ultimate remedy to the human dilemma is spiritual in nature. Beyond these similarities, however, there is little common ground between Hinduism and Christianity.

The differences, however, between these two religions are very great. In general, those who left Hinduism to follow Christ (myself included) appear to have done so for the very same reasons. These include the conviction that Hinduism offers a life of hopelessness, that a person is constantly having to depend on works, that there are too many gods, that Hinduism is associated with fear and guilt, and that there is no clear concept of sin.

Here are the main differences between Hinduism and Christianity in regards to the most important areas of life.

Religion

Hinduism is considered to be pantheistic as well as polytheistic. It is considered to be a pantheistic religion in that it assumes the supreme being, Brahman, is a non-personal presence which resides in everything around us. This kind of thinking supports the belief that the divine nature is united to all things. According to this belief system, divinity exists everywhere, and it identifies with the world. Hinduism is considered to be a polytheistic religion in that its deity is manifested in many forms as gods. In accordance with this religion, there are three supreme gods and many lesser deities having various levels or realms of authority.

Christianity's Biblical Response

A true Christian believer does not consider his belief system to be a religion, but rather a way of life. Furthermore, these believers view their belief system to be a personal relationship (one-on-one) between God and themselves. Other differences also exist which are dependent on the area of origin.

God

According to Hinduism, god is the impersonal, ultimate, but unknowable spiritual reality. Furthermore, this religion believes in a vast plurality of gods and goddesses as part of the impersonal Brahman. Hinduism holds to the prevailing belief in astrology, evil spirits, and curses and supports the worshipping of dead ancestors and religious teachers. The rationality behind this kind of thinking is that since God is in everything, then God is in both good and evil.

But if an individual ascribes to this belief, then he must also reconcile his thinking with the belief that there is no absolute morality, no divine law, and no divine being who will be discriminating between good and evil. This kind of thinking does not fit with the fact that Hinduism believes in worshipping the gods and goddesses in the form of images, idols, and statutes.

Christianity's Biblical Response

The Bible says that God is spirit (John 4:24) and is not flesh and blood (Matt.16:17). However, since individuals are made in the image of God, the characteristics of God are those of a living, personal Being. For example, as shown in the Christian Scriptures, God lives, He loves, He speaks, He works, He knows, He wills, and He sees. But God is not just an impersonal force, nor does He need a physical body in order to possess personal characteristics. God is a spirit and yet He possesses the characteristics of a personal individual. Thus the use of images in worship is forbidden. Exodus 20:4–5 states, "you shall not make any graven image nor bow down to such" (KJV). Since individuals are God's offspring, they should not think that the Godhead is like gold, silver, or stone graven by art or device of men (see Acts 17:29).

The Bible declares that there is only one God (Ephesians 4:5–6) and that He does not delight in destroying lives (see Ezekiel 33:11). God reveals Himself as Father, Son, and Holy Spirit. But, unlike Hindu deities, these three are one (as the Trinity) and are completely united in will, goals, and purposes.

Each person of the Trinity has complete authority over all aspects of creation. This belief is in direct contrast to that of Hinduism, which, for example, believes in a separate god over fire and a separate god over wealth. In accordance with Christian belief, each of these Persons is completely united in one God (John 17:20–21).

There is one God who cares deeply for each one of us as we read: "Hear, O Israel: The Lord our God, the Lord is one" (Deut. 6:4). We also read, "Call upon Me in the day of trouble; I will deliver you, and you shall glorify Me" (Ps. 50:15).

There is a five-fold difference between the incarnations of Vishnu and Jesus. First, Vishnu came to earth at least 9 times in which he took on both animal and human forms. Some Hindus believe that he came to earth much more frequently than this. Jesus came to earth only once in human form.

Second, while the core basis for stories of the avatars (or incarnations) of Vishnu might be truthful, their historical validation is not essential as they are primarily mythical in nature. One Hindu tradition even goes so far as to say that there were no footprints where the avatars walked. Conversely, the historical validation of Jesus' life is very important to the veracity of Jesus' claims and to the salvation that He accomplished on our behalf (1Cor. 15:14, 17). If Christ did not actually live, die, and rise from the dead, then the foundation of Christianity is built on a lie and the gospel is without merit.

Third, the whole purpose for Vishnu's incarnation was "for destruction of evil-doers" (Bhagavad-Gita-4:8). Conversely, the purpose for Jesus coming to earth was "to "seek and to save that which was lost" (Luke19:10, NKJV). "For God did not send His Son into the world to condemn the world, but to save the world through Him" (John 3:17, NKJV).

Fourth, the avatars revealed the way by which an individual can attain enlightenment over a period of many lifetimes: "But striving zealously, with sins cleansed, the disciplined man, perfected through many rebirths, then (finally) goes to the highest goal" (Bhagavad-Gita-6:45). Conversely, Jesus provided Himself as the way for an individual to immediately receive the gift of eternal life (John 6:29, 40).

Finally, Vishnu incarnates as an avatar over time as the need arises. The avatar dies and then goes back to inhabit the Brahman. In accordance with Hinduism, there are no claims of bodily resurrections of the avatars. Conversely, the incarnation of Jesus was a unique event. His sacrifice was a one-of-a-kind event, "once and for all" (see Hebrews 9:26–28). He died and rose from the dead; and His individual identity was maintained before His incarnation as well as after His incarnation.

Creation

Hindus accept various forms of pantheism and reject the Christian doctrine of creation. According to Hinduism, Brahman alone exists and everything else is an illusion (maya). It further believes that God emanated himself to cause the illusion of creation.

Moreover, this religion believes that there is no beginning or conclusion to creation, only endless repetitions of creation and destruction.

Hindus also believe that history has little value since it is based on an illusion. The world and everything in it are manifestations of Brahman. Thus, as related in the biblical sense, Hinduism has no concept of creation. According to Hindus, God forms physical beings either from things that already exist or from himself, but he does not create anything out of nothing.

Christianity's Biblical Response

The Christian doctrine states that God created the universe, the world, and everything in it (Genesis 1). As God did not create Himself, the world must exist in a separate form from God. Christianity affirms the reality of the material world and the genuineness of God's creation. The Bible declares that all is not God. God is present in His creation but He is not to be confused with it. Furthermore, the Bible contradicts pantheism by teaching creation rather than pantheistic emanation.

Man—Human Nature

Hindus believe that humans, as with all living things, are simply manifestations of Brahman. In accordance with this belief, an individual has no individual self, or self-worth. According to Eastern mysticism, individuality is an illusion. This kind of thinking supports the idea that an individual is not real and is not distinct from God or others. Accordingly, there is no separate ego, as all are one. Since individuality is only an illusion, then so is free will. If free will is only an illusion, then sin is also just an illusion.

If sin is just an illusion, then so is hell. According to Hinduism, the eternal soul (atman) of man is a manifestation of Brahman mysteriously trapped in the physical body. Furthermore, Hindus believe that gurus are a little lower than a god. Hindus also believe in religious leaders, named Brahmins, who use such tools as astrology, horoscopes, and Zodiac signs to direct the lives of their followers.

Christianity's Biblical Response

Christian doctrine states that man was made in the image of God with a personality and the ability to receive and give love. Although the image of God in man has been tarnished by the sin, man still has infinite value to God. This value was reinforced when God sent His only begotten Son, Jesus Christ, to die in order to redeem sinful man, even while man was still in rebellion against God.

Man is not divine. The apostle Peter refused to accept worship from Cornelius since Peter himself was a man (Acts 10:25–26). Furthermore, an individual's inner essence is not of God, thus it is not permissible to worship man, his ancestors, or religious teachers. When the people from Lystra began to offer a sacrifice to Paul and Barnabas because they thought they were gods, they were rebuked by these men of God who then told them to cease such practices and worship only the living God (Acts 14:15). The Bible says that man is a little lower than the angels (Ps.8:4–5; Heb. 2:6–9). God, also referred to as Yahweh, is against diviners and observers of times (Deut.18:10–14).

Sacred Texts

The Vedas are the most important of the Hindu writings. They were authored by an emerging priesthood, the Brahman caste, and have been preserved orally as well as in writing. But there are virtually no ancient manuscripts. How accurate these writings are makes little difference in terms of its adherents since they are not factual in content nor do they specify any historical events.

Christianity's Biblical Response

The four most sacred texts for many Hindus are the Vedas, Upanishads, Puranas, and most importantly, the Bhagavad-Gita. Here are some contradictions or discrepancies found in the Vedas as well as in the Bhagavad-Gita.

The Vedas

There existed incest among Hindu gods. The incest involved was between a brother and a sister or between a father and a daughter and can be read in the Rig Veda. Here are some examples:

1. In Rig-Veda-VI.55.4, (Apte-11), we read that Pushan is the lover of his sister.
2. In Rig-Veda-III.31.1-2, we read that father-daughter incest occurred in the famous story of Prajapati.
3. Because Prajapati has done something wrong, he was pierced by Agni (god of fire) as a punishment – (Sat.Br. XIII.9), (Apte-63).
4. In Rig-Veda-X.3.3, (Apte-11), we read that Agni (god of fire) was the lover of his own sister.
5. Ashvins (the twins) are born to Savitar and Ushas, who are brother and sister (Apte-11).
6. In Rig-Veda-I.116.19, we read that the Ashvins married Surya and Savitri, who were their sisters.
7. In Rig-Veda-I.91.7, we read that Agni (god of fire) is the son of his father and his sister.

Scientific Errors in the Vedas

There seem to be few scientific errors in the Vedas, especially in Rig-Veda as well as in Yajur-Veda. These errors were posted in the 'Hindu Forum' on: http:www.topix.com/forum/religion/hindu/ TTF4DU99P2NODJOPF.

Contradictions in The Bhagavad-Gita

The following articles address this issue:

1. Contradictions in Bhagavad-Gita by Vishwa Mohan. The article can be found at: www.VishwaMohan.com

2. Possible Difficulties in the Philosophy of the Bhagavad-Gita by Ernest Valea. The article can be found at: : http://www. comparativereligion.com/Gita.html

Sin

According to Hinduism, there is no sin against a holy god. Acts of wrongdoing are not targeted towards any god but come about mainly due to ignorance. These evil acts can be thwarted by following the guidelines of an individual's caste as well as by the way of salvation. In Hinduism, sin is committed against an individual's self as opposed to being committed against God. Since sin is committed only against an individual's self, the penalties of that sin are accrued only against an individual's self. The penalty for sin is the continuance of a repeated cycle of rebirths until an individual reaches Nirvana.

No salvation is needed since there is no sin, thus enlightenment is all that an individual needs. An individual does not need to be born again; rather, all he needs to do is recognize his inner divinity. If an individual is part of God, by definition he cannot be separated from God by sin. The Hindu religion teaches that humanity's problems stem from ignorance of unity with Brahman, desire, and violation of dharma (one's social duty).

Christianity's Biblical Response

The Christian doctrine states that sin is not due to ignorance of unity with Brahman but rather is a willful act of rebellion against God and His commandments (Eccl.7:20; Rom.1:28–32). The Bible declares, "All have sinned and fall short of the glory of God" (Rom.3:23, NKJV). The Christian doctrine recognizes sin to be an act of rebellion against a perfect and holy God. Furthermore, this doctrine goes on to say that all acts of transgressions are basically acts of rebellion against the laws of God.

The Bible states that "Against You, You only, have I sinned, and done this evil in Your sight—that You may be found just when You speak, and blameless when You judge" (Ps. 51:4, NKJV). Since sin cannot exist in the presence of God, the penalty for sin is spiritual death or separation from God. The Bible states that "the wages of sin is death" (Rom. 6:23). God gave us rules because He cares about us. He also gave individuals a free will so they can choose to disobey. But, disobedience (sin) is an offense against a holy God.

Karma

In accordance with the teachings of karma, each individual creates his own destiny by way of his thoughts, words, and deeds, and in keeping with the law of cause and effect. The Hindu gods do not forgive sins and are not interested in saving their devotees. If individuals do anything wrong, they have to face the karma that results from their actions whether or not they are sorry. Furthermore, karma teaches that everything that happens to an individual during his life, whether good or bad, comes about as a result of his or her conduct. "By doing good deeds in this life, therefore, one can improve his circumstances in the future, especially in future reincarnations" (Bhagavad-Gita).

Christianity's Biblical Response

The Bible states that through God's grace and favor lost sinners are delivered from any guilt, power, and eternal consequences resulting from their evil thoughts, words, and deeds. The God of the Bible is also full of mercy towards those who truly repent of their wrongdoing and turn to Him for forgiveness. God cancels the punishment that the individual would have otherwise received if he had not truly repented (Is. 38:1–6; Jonah 3).

In contrast to the doctrine of karma, the Bible teaches that men often do not receive their just reward for their lives while they are here on earth (Luke 16:19–25; Rom. 8:17–18). Instead, when Jesus returns, He will judge all men and declare their eternal rewards based on the type of life, good or bad, that they lived while here on earth. Thus, according to teachings in the Bible, any rewards or punishments an individual would receive for how he lived his life would come only after he has left earth.

Reincarnation

Hinduism teaches that the soul incarnates, that is, it evolves through many cycles of rebirths until all karmas have been resolved. It further teaches that all souls evolve towards union with God and will ultimately find spiritual knowledge and liberation from the cycle of rebirth. This destiny will eventually come about for all souls.

Hinduism also teaches that life is an endless cycles of rebirths. All living things die and then return in a different bodily form. Thus an individual's spirit is given another bodily form, such as that of an animal, person of another caste, or a god, in accordance with how that individual lived his current life. This cycle of death and rebirth continues until an individual is finally released. The Bhagavad-Gita states that, "as the embodied soul continually passes, in the body, from boyhood to youth to old age, the soul similarly passes into another body at death." (Gita-2:13).

Christianity's Biblical Response

The Bible teaches that "it is appointed for men to die once, and after this the judgment" (Heb.9:27, NKJV). The Hindu teaching of reincarnation also offers an appealing model for eternal life. But no proof can be given that any individual has ever lived and experienced reincarnation from an earlier life. Furthermore, there are such questions as, where do souls come from? And how are more souls created?

Another questionable aspect of reincarnation is the existence of a seemingly self-contradiction. The fundamental belief behind reincarnation is that over a number of death-rebirth cycles, an individual's soul gradually improves and becomes wiser and purer, allowing that person to ultimately reach moksha, or the unification with Brahman. In this state of oneness evil is conquered and all becomes good.

But Hinduism also teaches that all souls originated from Brahman. Thus, if the soul originated from Brahman to begin with, why would it need improvement through its cycles of rebirth? The soul is supposed to be pure and perfect as part of Brahman, so it would be against its nature to commit some evil that would reflect a need for improvement while united with Brahman.

Moksha—Liberation

The end goal of Hinduism is to be released from the cycle of reincarnation. An individual should seek to be set free from the cycle of birth, death, and rebirth so that he can exist in a pure state of impersonal spirit being without a physical body. When an individual becomes so attached to his physical existence, he loses sight of his true nature as a divine being. In order to be released, a person must somehow recognize himself for what he really is and act in keeping with his true self. He is to lose his attachment to his earthly existence.

The nature of this final state is not clearly defined. But Hinduism teaches that somehow an individual becomes part of the eternal being (Brahman). Some Hindus view the attainment of enlightenment as a state in which the individual losses consciousness; others view it as a state where they attain a sense of bliss. Thus Hindus believe that continuing to exist on earth is one form of punishment. Hindus believe that the attainment of eternal life is the state whereby an individual ceases to exist in a bodily form. In accordance with this belief, no concept of a bodily resurrection exists.

Christianity's Biblical Response

The Bible teaches that the whole human race was spiritually alienated from God when Adam sinned. It also teaches that those who are called by God and respond to His grace will receive the free gift of eternal life. Conversely, those who persist in rebellion against God will be lost for eternity. The Bible also teaches that an individual will come back in a glorified body, not as an animal, plant, insect, some other human being or a god. Thus, after death, an individual's spirit is reunited with his own body, as opposed to someone else's body (Matt. 22:23–33; Acts 24:15; John 11:24).

Salvation

Hinduism further teaches that salvation is the release from the wheel of life, the cycle of rebirths through which individuals must pass in order to better themselves and realize their attainment of oneness with Brahman. This process has to be worked out by each individual through successive lives. Hindus also believe that no particular religion teaches that there is only one way to salvation but that all genuine religious paths are facets of God's pure love and light and are deserving of tolerance and understanding.

Hindus believe that men are in need of salvation, that is, a release from the cycle of reincarnation to become gods. They also believe that this salvation can be achieved only through ceremonial works such as yoga or by getting a guru assigned to them. Hindus teach several ways by which this can be accomplished. Different methods to accomplish this are favored by various groups, but none of these groups rejects the methods that are taught by others. These methods include, but are not limited to, good deeds (karma), austerity and self-denial, knowledge, devotion, and meditation (yoga).

In general, Hindus do not refer to their ultimate goal as being salvation. Their hope or ultimate goal is that they are able to escape the reincarnation cycle and material existence. Hindus commonly refer to anything that pertains to leaving this material life or moving beyond it as being transcendental. The term transcendental can be repeatedly found in the introduction to the Bhagavad-Gita. The Hindu teaching on grace does not recognize the need for atonement of sin, but it simply offers forgiveness without any satisfaction for the judgment of sin that is required by a holy God.

Christianity's Biblical Response

In accordance with biblical teaching, however, an individual's spiritual need is for deliverance from God's judgment of his sin and restoration to a life under God's direction and care. The Bible also teaches that salvation can be provided only by God's gracious and undeserved action on behalf of the sinner. Thus, an individual's salvation is given by God as a free gift to all who will receive it and cannot be attained by good deeds. In other words, if an individual decides to receive this free gift he can attain eternal life or salvation by God's grace even though, according to his own merits, he deserves hell or eternal separation from God.

The Bible teaches that salvation is a gift from God through faith in Jesus Christ (Eph.2:8–10). The belief in reincarnation is in opposition to the teaching of the Bible (Heb. 9:27). Furthermore, the Christian's hope of eternal life means that all true believers in Christ will have a personal relationship with God. The Bible also teaches that it is impossible to earn an individual's salvation by performing good works (Titus3:3–7). Religious deeds and exercises are useless in terms of attaining salvation (Matt.7:22–23; Rom. 9:32; Eph. 2:8–9).

Furthermore, the Bible teaches that an individual is in need of salvation due to his own sins and that this salvation can come about only through faith in the Lord Jesus Christ. Those who receive Jesus as their Lord and Savior are saved and will one day receive a resurrected glorified body that will make them equal to the angels (Luke 20:36). According to the teachings of the Bible, man will never become a god. Jesus is God incarnate. He is the only sure path to salvation. Many religions offer ethical and spiritual insights, but only Jesus offers "the way, the truth, and the life" (John 14:6).

Salvation is a free gift to us from God; it cannot be earned. An individual, to receive this free gift, must accept it. Jesus bought man's salvation by taking all of man's sin upon Himself when He died on the cross. Thus He died as a sacrifice for mankind, and then rose from the dead three days later. Salvation gives man the right to spend eternity in heaven with the almighty God.

The gospel, or good news, states that God the Son became a man and died a sacrificial death on the cross, making a way possible for the forgiveness of man's sins against the true God. It is for those who place their complete trust in Christ. All individuals who do this can experience true forgiveness, know God and His purpose for their lives, and possess the certainty that they will have eternal life with Him.

The Conclusion

There are many differences between the Hindu religion and the Christian faith, and an individual can readily recognize that these two faiths can never come to terms or be reconciled. The basic foundations of each of these faiths are mutually exclusive. Christians believe that Hinduism cannot save because it worships the wrong god, follows the wrong religious authority, seeks the wrong destiny, and teaches the wrong ways to achieve that destiny.

Hinduism offers no objective evidence to support that their teachings were revealed by God or that their scriptures are truly divine. They may try to show that they are reasonable, but mainly they urge an individual to try it to see if he can find his religion to be satisfying. Hindus are usually very tolerant. Hindus are willing to tolerate (accept) almost anything.

Of the many religious documents in existence, the Bible is the only one that offers consistent reasonable evidence to convince the unbeliever that it is truly revealed by God. That evidence is found in such aspects as fulfilled prophecy, eyewitness testimony of miracles, and the resurrection of Christ. According to the Bible, only in Christ can an individual have the assurance of salvation.

A Final Note

Hindus should draw comfort in knowing that a greater hope exists. Indeed, it is more than a hope—it is an assurance. Hindus do not have to be relegated to endure a recycling of rebirth after rebirth in an attempt to get it right. They can be assured that there is a personal God who cares deeply for them. He knows how many hairs each individual has on his head, yet he controls every facet of the universe. God loves each individual and desires to redeem each person unto Himself. An indescribable joy awaits those who decide to accept God's Son as their Lord and Savior.

SECTION FOUR

CHRISTIANITY

CHAPTER 20

FACTS ABOUT
THE CHRISTIAN FAITH

THE BASIC TENETS of Christianity are rooted in Judaism. But the teachings of Jesus of Nazareth form the basis for the Christian faith. The name of Jesus is also that of "Christ." The Greek meaning of Christ is the "Anointed One," whereas the Hebrew meaning is the "Messiah." Christianity was first recognized as a separate faith in Judea, or modern-day Palestine, around A.D. 30 to 33. Over time, it has evolved to include many different denominations. Two reasons why so many denominations have evolved over the years include differences in teaching style and style of worship. But there is no evidence in the Bible that Jesus ever spoke or taught on anything related to denominations.

In his article *Don't All Spiritual Paths Lead to God?* author Steve Russo states, "Christianity isn't about people in search of God; rather it is about God in search of people." In the third chapter of John, Jesus states that an individual needs to be born again.

Despite denominational differences, most Christians agree on certain basic tenets of faith. The New Testament part of the Bible presents the story of Jesus Christ's ministry as well as the early history of Christianity.

Some Facts and Statistics

Christianity has the largest number of adherents, followed next in number by Islam and then Hinduism. Of the 6.5 billion people in the world, approximately 2.5 billion or one-third of these people identify with the Christian faith. Although many people these days may call themselves Christians, in truth not all are, as they may be Christians in name only. The Bible says that "many are called, but few chosen" (Matt. 20:16, NKJV).

The three major subcategories within Christianity include people who belong to the Eastern Orthodox Church, Roman Catholic Church, and those called Protestants. Of the total number of Christians, the people who belong to the Eastern Orthodox comprise about 15 percent, Protestants comprise about 22 percent, and Roman Catholics comprise about 53 percent. These three categories add up to 90 percent of the total number of Christians. Approximately 10 percent or about 230 million people may call themselves Christians but may not have an affiliation with any particular church, denomination, or organized Christian group.

Most members of the Eastern Orthodox Church are located in the Middle East or Eastern Europe. The Protestant churches include a number of denominations, such as Baptist, Episcopal, Lutheran, Methodist, Presbyterian, Pentecostal, and nondenominational. Of these, the Southern Baptist Convention is the largest body, which has about 25 million members. One author states that within each of these three major divisions, there are subdivisions or families of denominations.

A Short Introduction to Christianity

Christianity is unique, but it also shares some common beliefs with other world religions. For example, Christianity is a monotheistic religion. It teaches that there is just one God. The religions of Islam and Judaism also are monotheistic, but Islam calls God "Allah." Judaism believes in the same God as Christians, but they teach that their Messiah is yet to come.

Christianity also places a heavy emphasis on family relation-ships in a similar manner to that of the Mormon faith. The Bible teaches that followers of Jesus should meditate on and obey the teachings of Scriptures. Meditation is also important among those who follow the Hindu faith.

The difference that makes Christianity unique is the belief in Jesus as a person's Savior. Christians believe that Jesus, who is fully God, came to earth fully human to save those who were lost due to their sin and to offer Himself as a living sacrifice, or become a propitiation, for their sins. Thereby, He offers the free gift of eternal life to all who believe in Him. Other religions recognize Jesus as being a great teacher, a great prophet, an avatar of Vishnu, or one of many sons of God. But only Christianity identifies Jesus as being God as well as the only Son of God when He came to earth in human form.

Well-known theologian Francis Schaeffer once said, "True spirituality cannot be abstracted from truth at one end, nor from the whole man and the whole culture at the other. If there is a true spirituality, it must encompass all. The Bible insists that truth is one—and it is almost the sole surviving system in our generation that does."

Christianity is not just a religion or a way of life. Rather, it is all about a personal God who loves humanity (His creation) so much that He sent His only begotten Son (Jesus), who was without sin, to die on the cross in place of each individual to pay the price for his or her sin. That means that all persons can come to know God personally through the forgiveness of their sin and acceptance of Jesus as their Savior and in doing so receive the free gift of eternal life.

Most Christians believe that their faith is based solely on the life, death, resurrection, and teachings of Jesus Christ. Jesus per-sonally selected twelve disciples who spread the message of Jesus throughout the known world during the early church times. These twelve disciples included Simon (who is also named Peter), Andrew, James, John, Philip, Bartholomew, Mathew, Thomas, James, Simon (called Zelotes), Judas (brother of James), and Judas Iscariot (who betrayed Jesus) (see Luke6:14–16). The ministry of the apostles began right after the death, resurrection, and ascension of Jesus.

Although many people recognize Christianity as a religion, a true believer (one who is born again in Jesus, or saved) does not consider it to be a religion. Rather, Christians believe in a personal or one-on-one relationship with God. In order to attain this personal relationship, an individual does not have to engage in performing any religious works but believes in and confesses the finished work of Christ on the cross and in the resurrection.

Jesus Himself said twice in the third chapter of the Gospel of John that "one must be born again" (John 3:3, 7, NKJV). Other terms that can be used for being born again are saved, or redeemed, or child of God.

Central Beliefs

Most Christians agree on the following core beliefs:

1. The Bible is the inspired Word of God, given to many godly men under the unction of the Holy Spirit.
2. One God, manifested in three persons: God the Father, God the Son, and God the Holy Spirit. Christianity does not teach the belief that there are three gods, but rather one with three different manifestations.
3. God created the universe and yet is distinct from His creation. God created everything that is seen as well as unseen. He created all the people, animals, plants, insects, the world, and the angels. All the details about the creation can be found in the first book of the Bible, Genesis.
4. Every human who has ever lived was born a sinner and, thus, is separated from God. The Bible declares, "All have sinned and fall short of the glory of God" (Rom. 3: 23, NKJV). Jesus is the only exception, meaning He is the only one who is perfect and without sin.
5. Jesus is the Son of God and is one with God. He came to earth in human flesh to save us from our sins. In the Gospel

of John we read, "I and My Father are one" (John 10:30, NKJV).

6. Jesus was conceived of the Holy Spirit and was born to the Virgin Mary. The Bible declares: "Now the birth of Jesus Christ was on this wise: when as his mother Mary was espoused to Joseph, before they came together, she was found with child of the Holy Ghost" (Matt. 1:18).

7. Jesus suffered and died for our sins. He was falsely accused by the religious leaders such as the Pharisees and the Sadducees and, as explained in Mathew 27:23–56, He was brought before Pontius Pilate (the Roman governor) to be executed by crucifixion.

8. Jesus was crucified, buried, and was resurrected on the third day. There are at least twelve different accounts mentioned in the Bible where people saw Him after His resurrection. One of those references includes a large gathering of about 500 people witnessing His presence. Jesus rose from the dead (not reincarnated).

9. Once we are dead, it will be too late to decide to receive Jesus as Savior. It will not be possible. "It is appointed for men to die once, but after this the judgment" (Heb. 9: 27). Therefore one must choose to repent of his sin and accept Christ as his Lord and Savior before it is too late.

10. Anyone can be saved. The Bible confirms this statement both in John 3:16 and also in Romans 10:12. The notion of salvation is based purely on what God has done for us (by His grace) rather than on what we can do for Him (based on our works) (see Ephesians 2:8-9). Salvation is a free gift based on God's grace. We have to believe it and accept what Jesus did for us on the cross and in the resurrection.

11. Eternal life (called atman in Hinduism) does not mean that we travel from one body to the other. Rather, it means that the life the believers live is in Christ, who is eternal and gives eternal life. The Bible tells us that "to be absent from the body [is] to be present with the Lord" (2 Cor. 5:8). God

gives all of us free will, which means that we have the ability to either accept or reject Jesus.

The Trinity

Webster's Dictionary defines the term "Trinity" as, "The union of three divine figures, the Father, Son, and the Holy Ghost in one Godhead." The meaning of the term Trinity is considered by some to be somewhat confusing and is often thought of as being a mystery. How does the meaning of the Trinity fit with Christianity in the sense that it supports the belief in just one God?

Although the Trinity is all about the three-in-one nature of God, it is not even mentioned in the Bible. Yet, many Scriptures in both the Old and New Testaments refer to the concept of the Trinity. This concept supports the belief in one God with three manifestations or persons who are coequal and coeternal rather than a belief in three separate Gods.

Pat Robertson, President and CEO of CBN Ministry, in his book *Answers to 200 of Life's Most Probing Questions*, states that there are trinities in nature and that "light can be divided into three primary colors; yet light is one. A prism will reveal the individual colors separately that are unique yet unified." Some day, in God's timing, I believe that we will understand the mystery behind the Trinity as well as many other mysteries.

CHAPTER 21

THE TRINITY— GOD IN THREE PERSONS

THERE ARE AT least three Scripture verses in the Old Testament of the Bible that deal with the concept of the Trinity: Genesis1:1, Genesis 1:26, and Exodus 20:2–3. Ralph Muncaster, in his book *What Is Trinity?* states that the Hebrew word used for God (in Genesis and Exodus) is Elohiym. He further adds that the word Elohiym is plural.

But everywhere the word "God" is used in the Bible it is clearly talking about a supreme single God. Genesis 1:26 states, "And God said, Let us make man in our image, after our likeness...." The words "us" and "our" are plural in this Scripture, indicating that both words refer to the Trinity. The three divine persons or manifestations of the Trinity are the Father, the Son, and the Holy Spirit.

God, the Father

Who is the God of the Bible? The Bible describes God as follows: He is "eternal, all-powerful, all-knowing, personal spirit, who is everywhere-present, and who is the Creator and Sustainer of the universe. One of His primary attributes is holiness" (Rhodes, 2007). God is real and has a personality with real character.

The God of the Bible has both personal and spiritual characteristics. The Bible tells us that God is a Spirit: "God is a Spirit: and they that worship him must worship him in spirit and in truth" (John 4:24). The fact that God is not flesh and blood is confirmed by the scripture, "Blessed art thou, Simon Bar-jona: for flesh and blood hath not revealed it unto thee, but my Father which is in heaven" (Matthew-16:17).

Several Scriptures in the Bible portray God and His characteristics as that of a living, personal human being. God's characteristics can be summarized as: He knows, He lives, He loves, He sees, He speaks, He wills, and He works. All Scripture confirms that indeed God is personal and spirit-natured. Yet, He possesses the characteristics of a personal individual.

God is Eternal

God cannot be associated with the concept of time since He is eternal. The Bible states, "Before the mountains were brought forth, or ever thou hadst formed the earth and the world, even from everlasting to everlasting, thou art God" (Ps. 90:2). Furthermore, God is infinite; that is, He is far above and beyond His finite creation. Scripture states, "Now unto the King eternal, immortal, invisible, the only wise God, be honour and glory for ever and ever. Amen" (1 Tim.1:17).

God is Holy

God is perfect in all that He does, and He is also righteous. There is absolutely no evil that exists in Him; He is pure in everything He does. The Bible states, "And one cried unto another, and said, Holy, holy, holy, is the Lord of hosts: the whole earth is full of his glory" (Isa. 6:3). In addition, the Bible states, "Who shall not fear thee, O Lord, and glorify thy name? for thou only art holy: for all nations shall come and worship before thee; for thy judgments are made manifest" (Rev. 15:4).

God is Just

God is just. He will punish individuals for their sins. Although God forgives people of their sins when they request forgiveness, at the same time sin has consequence(s). Since God is just, He does not show favoritism nor is He partial towards any group or individual. He is fair to everyone and does not discriminate against anyone. The Bible states, "Then Peter opened his mouth, and said, Of a truth I perceive that God is no respecter of persons: But in every nation he that feareth him, and worketh righteousness, is accepted with him" (Acts 10:34–35).

God is Love

Not only is God's love perfect, but it is self-sacrificing. Even when individuals choose to rebel and sin against the holy and perfect God, He still loves them. He sent His only begotten Son (Jesus) to die for their sins. The Scripture states, "For God so loved the world, that he gave his only begotten Son, that whosoever believeth in him should not perish, but have everlasting life" (John 3:16).

God is Personal

The God of the Bible is a personal God, whereas those of other religions are impersonal. He is personally involved in His creation as well as in the lives of individuals to the extent that He even knows the number of hairs on our head (see Matthew 10:30). The God of the Bible also knows all individuals better than they know themselves. After all, He created each individual.

The Bible states, "O Lord, thou hast searched me, and known me. Thou knowest my downsitting and mine uprising, thou understandest my thought afar off. Thou compassest my path and my lying down, and art acquainted with all my ways. For there is not a word in my tongue, but, lo, O Lord, thou knowest it altogether" (Ps.139:1–4). Furthermore, the Bible states, "For thou hast possessed my reins: thou hast covered me in my mother's womb" (Ps.139:13).

God is Omnipotent

God is all-powerful. Thus no event, whether natural or supernatural, has any effect on Him. By his very nature as the Creator of the universe, He is much more powerful than any individual or anything and thus no individual or thing can successfully oppose Him. The Bible states, "But Jesus beheld them, and said unto them, With men this is impossible; but with God all things are possible" (Matt.19:26). It further adds, "And I heard as it were the voice of a great multitude, and as the voice of many waters, and as the voice of mighty thunderings, saying, Alleluia: for the Lord God omnipotent reigneth" (Rev. 19:6).

God is Omnipresent

God is omnipresent; that is, He is everywhere at the same time. But He is not present in everything, as is believed by Hindus to be the case with Hindu gods. Although the God of the Bible created the universe, He exists separately from His creation. The Bible states,

> Whither shall I go from thy spirit? or whither shall I flee from thy presence? If I ascend up into heaven, thou art there: if I make my bed in hell, behold, thou art there. If I take the wings of the morning, and dwell in the uttermost parts of the sea; Even there shall thy hand lead me, and thy right hand shall hold me. If I say, Surely the darkness shall cover me; even the night shall be light about me. Yea, the darkness hideth not from thee; but the night shineth as the day: the darkness and the light are both alike to thee.
>
> —Ps. 139:7–12

God is Omniscient

God is all knowing. In other words, He knows everything about an individual's past, present, and future. He even knows the thoughts of an individual before they are thought and He also knows all of the intentions, motives, and desires of each individual.

The Bible states, "For the ways of man are before the eyes of the Lord, and he pondereth all his goings" (Prov. 5:21).

God is Unchangeable

God does not change. Thus His promises always hold true. The Bible states, "I am the Lord, I change not" (Mal. 3:6). Furthermore, the Bible states, "Jesus Christ is the same yesterday, today, and forever" (Heb.13:8).

God has never separated Himself from His creation; therefore an individual can always gain access to Him through prayer. He created human beings so that He could fellowship with them and have a personal relationship with them. Authors Bickel and Jantz write, "God has spoken—meaning, He has revealed Himself to us in two distinct ways, namely, general revelation and special revelation" (Bickel & Jantz, 2002).

General Revelation

God's general revelation includes His creation that resides on earth as well as in the heavens (Ps. 19:1–2), and His moral laws and the truth about Himself (Rom. 1:19–20). The Bible states that God is a Spirit Being, making it difficult to prove His existence in a literal sense. But enough evidence is available to support the belief that He indeed is. All that an individual has to do is simply reflect on His creation to realize that it could not have been created by chance.

Special Revelation

God loves to have fellowship with His creation. Thus, He decided to give His Word (the Bible) to human beings. In the beginning, God spoke directly to people (Gen. 12:1). He also spoke through dreams (Gen. 20:6), through visions (Dan. 8:1), and also through angels (Acts 10:3). In addition to speaking through dreams, visions, and angels, He also inspired many writers who were given Scriptures while under the unction of the Holy Spirit. Thus, over a period of many years, these writers wrote and recorded God's personal message, otherwise known as the Holy Bible.

God's special revelation records events such as the parting of the Red Sea, inspiring men to write His message (2 Peter 1:21), and allowing His one and only Son to be incarnated as a man (John 1:14; Heb.1:1–2). God's special revelation declares the truth that human beings are spiritually dead, and, therefore, they are separated from God (Eph. 2:1).

There is not only good news, but hope. He has provided a plan for each individual to be saved (John 3:16; John 14:6; Acts 4:12; Rom. 10:13–17). We are given the opportunity to be reconciled with God, which can only come about through His Son, Jesus Christ.

God, the Son—Jesus

The second person of the Trinity is Jesus. Jesus is the eternal Son of God, and since He is one with God, He is also deity (John 1:1; John 8:58; Col. 2:9; Titus 2:13–14). The meaning of the name "Jesus" is "the Lord Saves." As stated by one Christian author, "In the incarnation, He took on a human nature so that He was 100 percent God and 100 percent man. As the God-man, He died on the cross as the Savior of humankind" (Rhodes, 2007). The Bible states, "For when we were yet without strength, in due time, Christ died for the ungodly" (Rom. 5:6).

Jesus was born to a devout Jewess named Mary who was engaged to a Jewish carpenter named Joseph from Nazareth in Galilee. Jesus was born in the Roman province of Palestine, also known as present-day Israel, sometime around 6 B.C. Although this date is probably fairly accurate, there are some variations on the timing of His birth.

The reason this date is considered to be fairly accurate is that Herod the Great died in 4 B.C., and Herod was still alive at the time Jesus was born (Matt. 2:1; Luke 1:5). Furthermore, Herod decreed that all firstborn male babies under the age of two be killed. Author Mark Water stated, "Jesus was probably a toddler when the wise men visited Him and Herod was still alive then" (Water, 1999).

Jesus was born in a stable since it was the only place available at the time and most likely Joseph and Mary could not have afforded a better place. Jesus was born to Mary, who was a virgin at the time, and thus Jesus was conceived by the Holy Spirit. Therefore, Jesus' birth to the Virgin Mary was a miracle. Furthermore, several hundred years before the birth of Jesus, the prophet Isaiah had prophesied Jesus' birth: "Therefore the Lord himself shall give you a sign; Behold a virgin shall conceive, and bear a son, and shall call his name Immanuel" (Isa. 7:14).

The New Testament confirms this event. It states that one day an angel of the Lord appeared to the young virgin named Mary. It further states, "And the angel answered and said unto her, The Holy Ghost shall come upon thee, and the power of the Highest shall overshadow thee: therefore also that holy thing which shall be born of thee shall be called the Son of God" (Luke 1:35).

The angel told Mary that she would give birth to a son and that He would be the Messiah. One author writes, "This is the way God entered into humanity to bring a second Adam. God the Son enfleshed Himself" (Robertson, 1984). This is why Jesus is called the Son of God, as well as the Son of man, since He was born to Mary who was a human being.

Jesus is often referred to as the Christ. This term is generally thought to indicate his title. It is derived from the Greek word "xristos," which translates to *the anointed one*. Author Robert Pollock states, "It has the same meaning as 'meshiach' or 'messiah' in Hebrew." Jesus was also referred to as "Jesus of Nazareth."

Jesus: Names and Titles

Jesus identified Himself with many titles. An individual can gain a lot of revelatory information about Jesus by considering these titles. These titles of Jesus (the great I AM) are provided below for consideration.

1. Resurrection and the life – John 11:25
2. Bread of life – John 6:35, 48, 51

3. Light of the world – John 8:12
4. I AM – John 8:58 (NKJV)
5. Good shepherd – John 10:11, 14
6. Son of God – John 10:36
7. The Way, the Truth, and the Life – John 14:6
8. Alpha and the Omega, the beginning and the end – Revelation 1:8; 21:6; 22:13
9. The first and the last – Revelation 22:13
10. The root and offspring of David – Revelation 22:16

Divine Titles of Christ

Jesus, based on His deity, is also known by the following titles.

1. Wonderful, Counselor, Mighty God, Everlasting Father, Prince of Peace – Isaiah 9:6-7
2. God with us and Immanuel – Matthew 1:23 (NKJV)
3. Lord and Christ –Acts 2:36
4. Christ the Lord – Luke 2:11
5. The Son of God – Matthew 4:3; John 1:34
6. The Word of God – Revelation 19:13
7. King of kings and Lord of lords – Revelation 19:16

The Early Years

For the most part, there are very few details providing information about the early years of Jesus when He was growing up. There were reports of His activities around the time He was eleven or twelve years of age, and then no reports were written until He reached thirty years of age. But the Bible states that Jesus followed after the footsteps of His father (Joseph) in that He became a professional carpenter.

According to the Gospel of Luke, Jesus visited the temple and was interacting with the religious teachers when He was about twelve. When Mary asked Jesus about this visit, Jesus said that He was minding His Father's business. The next account of Jesus was not given until He presented himself as a teacher when He was around thirty. His entire ministry lasted about three and one-half years, thus He must have been around thirty-three at the time of his crucifixion.

Jesus spoke Hebrew but He also spoke Aramaic, a Semitic language which has close ties to the Hebrew language. Jesus also spoke Greek, the main trade language at that time and the language He used to converse with the Roman officials. Many people during this time were most likely fluent in both Aramaic and Greek. The New Testament of the Bible was written in Greek.

His Teaching and Healing Ministry

Jesus taught and healed many times during the approximate three-and-one-half years of His ministry while here on earth. During this time He primarily taught on the kingdom of God and often used parables to present His teachings. The religious leaders, or Pharisees and Sadducees, often practiced the religious hypocrisy that was so prevalent at that time. Jesus frequently rebuked this kind of hypocrisy.

He chose to place the focus of His ministry on the importance of love, compassion, kindness, forgiveness, and mercy to everyone, including an individual's enemies. The most famous teaching that He delivered was the Sermon on the Mount, a teaching that primarily focused on real-life principles. This teaching stressed the importance of selflessness, or not being self-centered, as well as maintaining a spirit of repentance.

Jesus also performed many miracles, such as when He turned water into wine, walked on water, calmed the raging storm, cursed a fig tree, healed the sick, fed thousands with very little food, cast out demons, and raised a dead man named Lazarus from the dead. As Jesus rapidly gained in popularity, many people developed a strong opposition to Him, in particular the local religious Jewish leaders. The fact that Jesus identified himself as the King and the Messiah made these leaders increasingly uncomfortable.

Betrayal and Crucifixion

The Gospels consistently state that Jesus frequently told His disciples that His end was near, but they did not understand or accept this message. During the Last Supper, which was the night before His death, Jesus attempted to clarify what He had meant when He gave this message. All four of the Gospels state how Jesus shared the bread, which represented His body, and the wine, which represented His blood.

During the Last Supper Jesus prophesied that one of the twelve disciples would betray Him. This disciple, Judas Iscariot, did so by leading the Roman soldiers to the place where Jesus was and telling these soldiers to arrest the man whom he would kiss. Judas received thirty pieces of silver as payment for this betrayal. The Bible relates that Judas threw all thirty pieces on the floor of the temple and committed suicide by hanging himself.

Jesus was brought before the Jewish chief priest for trial. Although Jesus said very little during His trial, He did claim to be the Messiah. Thus the Jewish leaders accused Jesus of blasphemy. He was handed over to Pontius Pilate, the Roman governor of Judea, for judgment and sentencing for this crime.

Although Pontius Pilate did not find any fault with Jesus, he sentenced Him to death out of fear of the rebellious mob and also to quiet that crowd. In accordance with the custom of that time, one prisoner would be allowed to be released per year. But this angry mob demanded that Jesus be put to death by crucifixion and requested that a well-known criminal named Barabbas be released instead of Jesus.

Jesus was badly beaten, whipped, and forced in a demeaning manner to wear a purple robe and crown of thorns that gave Him the appearance of being a king. He was executed by crucifixion on Golgotha, a hill also known as the place of a skull. His crucifixion entailed a process in which long nails were driven into both of His hands and feet, thus affixing His body to a wooden cross. This eventually led to His slow and painful death. Even while enduring this painful ordeal, Jesus prayed to His Father God to "forgive them; for they know not what they do" (Luke 23:34).

Empty Tomb and Resurrection

After Jesus died, His body was removed from the cross and placed in a tomb carved out of solid rock that was owned by Joseph of Arimathea. After three days and nights, Jesus' mother and one or two other women came to the tomb to anoint His body with spices. When they reached the tomb, they were surprised to find that the stone that was covering the tomb was rolled away and the tomb was empty (Matthew 28:1–10).

The women told the disciples what they saw when they went to visit the tomb, but the disciples refused to believe their story. Nevertheless, the risen Lord appeared to the disciples later although He had not yet received His glorified body.

The Bible clearly describes the appearance of Jesus to both men and women on at least twelve different occasions. Approximately 500 people witnessed the resurrected Jesus on one of those occasions (Luke 24:13–32, 34). After the resurrection of Jesus, He ascended to heaven to sit at the right hand of God's throne. Jesus' resurrection is a critical aspect of the Christian faith.

God the Holy Spirit

The Holy Spirit is also known as the third person of the Trinity, or the Holy Ghost. This term is mentioned throughout the Old Testament of the Bible. For example, the book of Genesis states, "And the earth was without form, and void; and darkness was upon the face of the deep. And the Spirit of God moved upon the face of the waters" (Gen. 1:2).

Involvement of the Holy Spirit is clearly indicated from the start of creation. Furthermore, the role of the Holy Spirit was not described as being significantly different in either the Old or New Testaments of the Bible. Although there may be some differences between the descriptions of the Holy Spirit in these two testaments, the unity between these two testaments remains the same.

The role of the Holy Spirit as described in the Old Testament is that of a counselor and helper. For example, the Bible states, "And I have filled him with the spirit of God, in wisdom, and in understanding, and in knowledge, and in all manner of workmanship" (Ex. 31:3). Furthermore, the book of Numbers 24:2–3 clearly indicates that there are some who reject God and yet were inspired by the Holy Spirit "as indicated by the pagan prophet Balaam's blessings of Israel despite the enemy king Balak's attempts to purchase a curse" (Muncaster, 2004).

God the Holy Spirit will never lead anyone in a way that is contradictory to the Word of God. To do so would in essence be like God acting in opposition to Himself. Some Christians choose to sin and then try to convince themselves that the Holy Spirit gave them peace about that situation and confirmed to them that their action was not sinful. For example, two individuals may choose to live together as a couple but are not married while professing all the while to be born-again Christians. They deceive themselves into thinking there is nothing wrong with what they are doing so that they may selfishly fulfill their lust for each other. Another example is when individuals choose to abort their unborn infant because, selfishly, they decide that they are not quite ready to become parents. These two scenarios are representative of mankind at his worst. The Bible states, "And grieve not the Holy Spirit of God, whereby ye are sealed unto the day of redemption" (Eph. 4:30).

Some professing believers have told me that the Holy Spirit gave them permission to do certain things which God very clearly prohibits in His Word. How can this seeming contradiction hold true? It is no wonder that Scripture states, "believe not every spirit, but try the spirits whether they are of God" (1 John 4:1). How is the spirit tested? The best way to do this is to compare each statement against the Word of God as the standard.

The Holy Spirit plays a major role in the life of a Christian believer. One Christian author describes the Holy Spirit as follows: "He inspires people to: build, speak, preach, laugh, sing, and make music. Furthermore, the Holy Spirit helps us to: pray, repent, become humble, and yield stubborn wills. He gives: courage, leadership, visions, divine revelation, dreams, true reverence for God" (Waters, 1999).

The Bible relates that there are nine fruits of the Spirit and nine gifts of the Spirit. The nine fruits of the Spirit are: love, joy, peace, longsuffering, gentleness, goodness, faith, meekness, and temperance (Gal. 5:22–23). The nine gifts of the Spirit are the word of wisdom, word of knowledge, faith, gifts of healing, working of miracles, prophecy, discerning of spirits, diverse kinds of tongues, and interpretation of tongues (see 1 Cor. 12:8–10). These nine gifts are classified into three categories, including gifts of power, revelatory gifts, and gifts of utterance. As a general rule, the gifts of the Spirit are often emphasized mostly by churches or individuals who identify with the charismatic or Pentecostal movement.

The Trinity in the New Testament

The concept of the Trinity is described throughout the New Testament of the Bible. The ministry of Jesus first began with His baptism by John the Baptist. At the time of this event, each manifestation of the Trinity was revealed. One Christian author (Muncaster, 2004) described the detailed account of this event as follows:

The Son was humbly submitting Himself in human form to the Father, as a model for all of the world (Matt. 3:15).

The Father spoke from heaven, saying, "This is my beloved Son, in whom I am well pleased" (Matt. 3:17).

The Holy Spirit—the Spirit of God descended like a dove, and lighted upon Jesus (Matt. 3:16).

Jesus gave His disciples some specific instructions towards the end of His ministry. The Bible states, "Go ye therefore, and teach all nations, baptizing them in the name of the Father, and of the Son, and of the Holy Ghost" (Matt. 28:19). These specific instructions are also known as the Great Commission.

The concept of the Trinity has not only been described in the beginning and end of Jesus' ministry but at other times as well. For example, as Jesus was speaking to Phillip He said, "And I will pray the Father, and he shall give you another Comforter [Holy Spirit], that he may abide with you forever" (John 14:16).

The apostle Paul has also described the three-in-one nature of God (1 Cor.12:4–6). Furthermore, the Gospel of John clearly reveals that Jesus takes on the role of an intercessor, the Holy Spirit acting as the believer's helper in his day-to-day living (John 14:16–17).

CHAPTER 22

THE BIBLE—
THE WORD OF GOD

THE BIBLE IS divided into two distinct testaments known as the Old and New Testaments. The Old Testament is written in Hebrew and the New Testament is written in Greek. The Bible consists of sixty-six books, thirty-nine of which make up the Old Testament and twenty-seven are in the New Testament. According to the New Testament Scriptures, all biblical writings are inspired, meaning God-breathed by the Holy Spirit.

These Scriptures state, "All scripture is given by inspiration of God, and is profitable for doctrine, for reproof, for correction, for instruction in righteousness" (2 Tim. 3:16) and "For the prophecy came not in old time by the will of man: but holy men of God spake as they were moved by the Holy Ghost" (2 Peter 1:21). Furthermore, the Scriptures reveal that God's Word is inerrant and infallible: "If he called them gods, unto whom the word of God came, and the scripture cannot be broken" (John 10:35).

Although the Bible provides in-depth knowledge that extends beyond any one individual's human comprehension, it is a book that relates divine revelation about God. There are many ways that God communicates with humans. For example, He speaks to humans through His creation, including other individuals, nature, and even animals. But the primary way He communicates is through His Word, the Bible.

The Bible is complete in that it covers every challenge or issue that pertains to life from early childhood through old age. Furthermore, it provides specific instructions on how an individual should live on a daily basis. It also provides information that can assist individuals in comprehending relationships and friendships, including those between husband and wife, parents and children, and employer and employee.

Although humans were created in God's image, they possess only a finite mind, whereas God, being divine, possesses an infinite and supernatural mind. Thus it is not always easy for humans to grasp an understanding of the supernatural aspects of God. But the Bible contains divine revelation concerning the mysteries of God.

For example, the Bible states, "Canst thou by searching find out God? Canst thou find out the Almighty unto perfection? It is as high as heaven; what canst thou do? Deeper than hell; what canst thou know? The measure thereof is longer than the earth, and broader than the sea" (Job 11:7–9).

The Word of God, or the Bible, is compared to a lamp, a light, bread, fire, hammer, honey, meat, milk, seed, spiritual food, sword, and water. God used a variety of ways to communicate to the writers of the Bible, including angels, a donkey, dreams, visions, voices, and world events. Furthermore, sometimes He even spoke directly: "The Spirit of the Lord spake by me, and his word was in my tongue" (2 Sam. 23:2).

Although the Bible is the Word of God and is, thus, God inspired, it is also the word of men since God spoke through men (human authors) as they were inspired by the Holy Spirit. This statement is supported by two Scriptures. First, the Bible states, "For the mouth of the Lord has spoken it" (Isa. 1:20). And it also states, "God, who at sundry times and in divers manners spake in time past unto the fathers by the prophets" (Heb. 1:1). Thus Scripture in its entirety is God's Word that was written by man but declares exactly what God specified, nothing less and nothing more.

In the book *The Bible Made Plain and Simple*, author Mark Water provides help for individuals to be able to comprehend the question, "What did God want to achieve (or accomplish) through the Scriptures?" He furthermore explains the following:

1. To make Jesus' testimony known (John 5:39).
2. To make us holy, separate, sanctified, and set apart (John 17:17).
3. To give us spiritual life (James 1:18).
4. To produce faith (Rom. 10:17).
5. To search our hearts (Heb. 4:12).
6. To make us wise (Ps. 19:7).
7. To give victory over Satan (Eph. 6:11, 17).
8. To give us examples to follow and warnings to heed (1 Cor. 10:11).
9. To make us wise concerning salvation (2 Tim. 3:15).

Old Testament of the Bible

The Old Testament includes thirty-nine books that speak about the history of the Jews, as well as their religious customs and rituals. These books are further sub-classified into five sections, including the Pentateuch or Torah, historical books, poetical books, major prophets and minor prophets. The length of the text in the major and minor prophets is the primary difference between prophetical books, and thus this difference has nothing to do with one being superior over the other.

Most scholars agree that Moses authored all five books of the Pentateuch. These five books focus primarily on such issues as descendants, redemption, holiness, wanderings, and remembering. The 12 historical books of the Bible relate the story of Israel; that is, they trace the history of the Israelites from their entry into Canaan, the two kingdoms of Israel and Judah being overthrown, their captivity in foreign lands, and their eventual homecoming.

The five poetical books of the Bible are further categorized into three subtypes, including didactic, lyric, and dramatic. Christian author, Mark Water, describes these types of poetry as follows: "Didactic poetry is teaching about life from maxims (Proverbs and Ecclesiastes), lyric poetry is originally accompanied by a lyre (most of the Psalms), and dramatic poetry is a dialogue in poetic form (Job and Song of Solomon)."

Although the Bible acknowledges both the major and minor prophets, there appears to be a third type of prophet known as oral prophets. The Old Testament describes several prophets who did not leave any written records and yet the existence of their presence has survived. Elijah is just one of many oral prophets. Other such examples include Azariah, Elisha, Iddo, Jahaziel, Jehu, and Nathan.

Although the major and minor prophets may differ in terms of the length of their books, they have four prophetic themes in common that speak for all of their books. These themes include the following: 1) all of the prophets exposed people's sinful actions, 2) the prophets spoke to the people to repent and to follow after God's laws, 3) the prophets warned people about God's coming judgment, and 4) the prophets expectantly looked for the coming of the Messiah.

The prophets' primary purpose was to bring forth God's light to a dark and dying world, as stated in the Bible, "And so we have the prophetic word confirmed, which you do well to heed as a light that shines in a dark place, until the day dawns and the morning star rises in your hearts" (2 Peter 1:19). Thus, the prophecies in the Bible revealed the Word of God whether or not the subject matter pertained to the past, present, or future.

The Old Testament of the Bible describes the captivity of the Jews while they were in Babylonia, as well as their history, and ends with the return of the remnant from their captivity. There are a total of seventeen prophetic books of which "twelve books refer to the time before captivity, two books refer to the time during the captivity, and three books refer to the time after the captivity" (Water, 1999).

What can an individual learn from the Old Testament? The answer to this question is, "a lot." The Old Testament covers the redemptive history of the Israelites. It describes how God has acted on behalf of His people and also relates the role of God in the redemption of this world. Strangely, many Christians these days are concerned only about the New Testament, as they believe that the Old Testament is no longer relevant.

Other Christians have convinced themselves that there are two different gods, one being the God of the Old Testament and the other being the God of the New Testament. The underlying reason for this disconnect is probably due to the different role that God plays in the Old Testament versus that which He plays in the New Testament. For example, in the Old Testament, God is portrayed as a God of anger, justice, holiness, and wrath. In the New Testament, God is portrayed as a God of forgiveness, grace, love, and mercy.

But, God never changes. He is the same today, yesterday, and forever. He is the same God in both the Old and New Testaments. The famous theologian, R. C. Sproul, once stated, "The Old is in the New revealed; the New is in the Old concealed" He was quoting St. Augustine. In his book *Now, That's a Good Question*, R. C Sproul states that "about three-fourths of the information in the New Testament is either a quotation of, an allusion to, or a fulfillment of something that was already founded in the Old Testament."

The Old Testament, also known as the Hebrew Bible, speaks primarily of Jewish history and prophecies. The Jewish religion, or Judaism, and its influence in the Western culture are considered to be of great importance since the roots of Christianity stem from this religion. The writers of the Old Testament clearly specify that they were communicating God's Word when they used such phrases as, "thus says the Lord" and "the Word of the Lord came to me." The Scriptures that confirm these statements include:

"And the Lord said unto Moses, Write thou these words: for after the tenor of these words I have made a covenant with thee and with Israel" (Ex. 34:27).

"All this, said David, the Lord made me understand in writing by His hand upon me, even all the works of this pattern" (1 Chron. 8:19).

"And it came to pass in the fourth year of Jehoiakim the son of Josiah king of Judah, that this word came unto Jeremiah from the LORD, saying, take thee a roll of a book, and write therein all the words that I have spoken unto thee" (Jer. 36:1–2).

The Purpose of the Old Testament

The primary purpose of the Old Testament is to point to the person of Jesus, the coming Redeemer and His work. The Bible clearly states that the Old Testament Scriptures are all about Jesus, and this is also confirmed in the New Testament, "And beginning at Moses and all the prophets, he expounded unto them in all the scriptures the things concerning himself" (Luke 24:27).

The New Testament

The New Testament consists of twenty-seven books that are divided into the following subcategories: the Gospels, history, the letters of Paul, letters written by other apostles and apocalyptic writings. There are four Gospels (Matthew, Mark, Luke, and John), one book in the history category; thirteen letters written by the apostle Paul, one letter that is attributed to Paul, seven letters written by other apostles, and one book of apocalyptic writing written by the apostle John.

Interestingly, the word "sea" takes on an important position in the New Testament. For example, both the early and late ministry of Jesus is closely connected with the sea. In addition, many of Paul's journeys were taken by sea. The Bible clearly states that many of Jesus' miracles occurred on or near the sea. For example, He calmed a storm (Matt. 8:23–27), walked on the water (Mark 6:48–51), and increased the fishing catch of His disciples (Luke 5:4–11; John 21:1–11). Furthermore, the place where the famous Sermon on the Mount was delivered was located at Capernaum, near the Sea of Galilee.

The Mediterranean Sea was the place where many key events took place for the disciples, the apostles Paul and John. The Mediterranean Sea was used as a means of travel in order to spread the word of Jesus after His death and resurrection. In addition, many of the places where Paul preached were located along the coastal regions. Furthermore, the apostle John was exiled on the island of Patmos where he wrote the book of Revelation.

The best way to learn about Jesus is to look at the Scriptures that deal with what He said about Himself. There are many Scriptures in each of the four Gospels where Jesus teaches about Himself. Who is Jesus in the Gospels? Jesus is portrayed in different ways by each of the four Gospel writers. Jesus is portrayed as the King in the Gospel of Matthew. He is portrayed as Servant in the Gospel of Mark. He is portrayed as Man in the Gospel of Luke. He is portrayed as God in the Gospel of John.

The Word of God, or the Bible, is truth, and there are many ways to establish its credibility. In his book *Christianity for Skeptics,* Steve Kumar defended the Bible on the basis of five solid grounds, which will establish beyond any shadow of doubt that the Bible is indeed the Word of God. The five areas that he presents include archaeology, history, Jesus Himself, prophecy, and reason.

CHAPTER 23

THE CHURCH

W HEN INDIVIDUALS BECOME believers in Christ and accept Him into their hearts they become born-again persons in their spirit and a member of the body of Christ, also known as the church. The local church is where believers come together to study God's Word, worship, and receive God's message delivered from the pulpit. Although many believers use the church as a gathering place, many churches have an open-door policy in that all individuals are welcome regardless of their affiliation with a particular denomination and whether or not they are believers or nonbelievers.

As stated in the Bible, many churches practice unity yet diversity in the body, "For by one Spirit are we all baptized into one body, whether we be Jews or Gentiles, whether we be bond or free; and have been all made to drink into one Spirit. For the body is not one member, but many" (1 Cor. 12:13–14).

Author Phillip Yancey asks the question, why are there so many more professing Christians than church-going Christians? In his book *Church: Why Bother?* he describes how difficult it is to sort out the human failings of the local churches from the perfect church that is without spot or wrinkle and represents the body of Christ. Many individuals appear to agree with Mr. Yancey.

A huge disparity exists between what is ideal versus what is real. Although the local church fulfills an important purpose, the disagreements and petty arguments that seem to separate one church from another can be very frustrating as well as disappointing.

What is the Church?

The church in its earliest form was in existence before the formation of the many denominational churches. Despite the formation of these churches, spiritually speaking, there is still just one church. Author Wayne Grudem defined the church as "the community of all true believers for all time." (Grudem, 1994). Authors Bickel and Jantz further defined the church as, "Community is important to God. In effect, God exists in community through the Trinity, and God created us in His image to be in community first with Him and then with each other" (Bickel & Jantz, 2002).

The concept of the church originated before the time of Jesus, although Jesus played a key role in developing a new community of believers that was comprised of both Jews and Gentiles (non-Jews). The old covenant was an agreement between God and His people, or the Jews. In contrast, the new covenant is an agreement between God and all who accept Christ into their hearts and make Him their Lord and Savior regardless of their being Jews or Gentiles.

At one time, the apostle Paul was considered to be the greatest enemy of the church. But, once Paul was converted, he became a great servant of Christ as well as the greatest missionary in the world. In the Bible, Paul described the church, also known as body of Christ, as follows: "For as the body is one, and hath many members, and all the members of that one body, being many, are one body; so also is Christ. For by one Spirit are we all baptized into one body, whether we be Jews or Gentiles, whether we be bond or free; and have been all made to drink into one Spirit" (1 Cor. 12:12–13).

All individuals who are true believers, that is, those who have committed their lives to Jesus Christ, have been called as missionaries. But, individuals often misunderstand the calling of a missionary. They envision a missionary as someone who constantly travels and lives in a remote village or jungle. But this is not always the case. Individuals are often called to become missionaries right at the place where they first come to know Jesus as their personal Lord and Savior. In this sense, the mission field may be right in an individual's back yard or place of work. Jesus called every true believer to become a missionary when He stated, "But you shall receive power, after that the Holy Ghost is come upon you: and ye shall be witness unto me both in Jerusalem, and in all Judea, and in Samaria, and unto the uttermost part of the earth" (Acts 1:8).

Authors Bickel and Jantz provide a detailed explanation of how the modern church got started: "Within 50 days of this commission (from Jesus), the Holy Spirit came upon the believers in power, just as Jesus had predicted, and the church we know today was born." (Bickel & Jantz, 2002). After its inception, individual believers and groups went forth to various locations as they were directed by the Holy Spirit to deliver the gospel or message of Christianity to people throughout the earth.

For example, Thomas, one of the disciples of Jesus, may have traveled as far as India to help spread the gospel of Christ. Indeed, some records show that he preached in Chennai, a southern city in India, where he was killed by a spear that was thrust into his back. He was reported to have given his life for Christ. In like manner, other disciples have also traveled to distant locations such as Asia to help spread the gospel of Christ.

Many Denominations

There are three major divisions within Christianity. These divisions include Eastern Orthodoxy, Protestantism, and Roman Catholicism. The roots of Eastern Orthodoxy stem from what was the Eastern Roman Empire or somewhere around the Middle Eastern region. The roots of Protestantism stem from the religious protests of the 1500s. Within Protestantism there are many subdivisions, or families of denominations. Roman Catholicism is under the authority and leadership of the Bishop of Rome (the Pope).

Rituals and Customs

Several common rituals and customs that are practiced in Christianity include baptism, communion or the Lord's Supper, confirmation, prayer, marriage, and burial.

Man-Humanity

The Bible states that God created all human beings in His image (Gen. 1:26) and that they are created a little lower than the angels (Ps. 8:3–6). The Bible also states that humans possess both a physical body and a spiritual soul (1 Peter-2:11). Although human beings are all created in God's image, they all have at some time chosen to sin. Sin by its very definition is any act of rebellion against a holy and righteous God. The Bible states, "For all have sinned and fall short of the glory of God" (Rom. 3:23). It also declares, "For the wages of sin is death; but the gift of God is eternal life through Jesus Christ our Lord" (Rom. 6:23).

Although there are many severe consequences of sin, the most debilitating is that it separates individuals from God. The Bible states, "But your iniquities have separated between you and your God, and your sins have hid his face from you, that he will not hear" (Isa. 59:2). Furthermore, the Bible states, "Thou art of purer eyes than to behold evil, and canst not look on iniquity: wherefore lookest thou upon them that deal treacherously, and holdest thy tongue when the wicked devoureth the man that is more righteous than he?" (Hab.1:13). Sin for a season may give pleasure, but it may take many years to restore a life that has been ravaged by sin.

The eventual consequence of sin is that it brings forth spiritual death. At some time during their life, individuals are not only subject to a physical death but they are also subject to a spiritual death. Physical death takes place when the spirit part of the human being becomes separated from the physical part of the body. In a likewise manner, spiritual death takes place when individuals become separated from God. The apostle Paul discussed this issue when he stated, "And you hath he quickened, who were dead in trespasses and sins" (Eph. 2:1).

Although man is often considered to be divine by other religions, such as Hinduism, the Bible clearly refutes this. The Bible states that although man is created in the image of God (Gen. 1:26), he is not divine. Thus the inner man is not the same as that of God's inner being. Individuals are not meant to be worshipped, as they are not on the divine level as is God. The Bible further states that it is considered blasphemous to believe that a human being has a divine nature.

The disciple, Peter, refused to accept worship from Cornelius because he considered himself to be a mere man. The Bible states, "And as Peter was coming in, Cornelius met him, and fell down at his feet, and worshipped him. But Peter took him up, saying, stand up; I myself also am a man" (Acts 10:25–26).

The Bible also states that God is not a man (see 1 Samuel-15:29). Furthermore, the Bible states that when the people of Lystra began worshipping and treating Paul and Barnabas like gods, these men instructed them to cease doing so and instead to worship only the living God. The Bible states, "And saying, Sirs, why do you these things? We also are men of like passions with you, and preach unto you that you should turn from these vanities unto the living God, which made heaven, and earth, and the sea, and all things that are therein" (Acts 14:15). Thus, since our inner being is not divine like that of God, it is not appropriate to worship any man, ancestors, or religious teachers and leaders.

In addition, the Bible teaches that man has only one earthly life and death and cannot reincarnate himself. "It is appointed unto men once to die, but after this the judgment" (Heb. 9:27). When a believer dies, his soul does not travel from body to body. Instead, his physical body returns to dust and the spiritual part of the person returns to God. "Then shall the dust return to the earth as it was: and the spirit shall return unto God who gave it" (Eccl. 12:7).

When human beings die, their destiny has already been decided. They will either be going to heaven or hell, based on whether or not they had accepted Christ into their heart during their lives. The Bible states that man does not have the ability to change his destiny from one of suffering to one of bliss and vice versa (See Luke 16:26).

Many individuals have questioned God's purpose for man. The Bible states that God gave a command for men to "be fruitful and multiply; fill the earth and subdue it; have dominion…" (Gen. 1:28, NKJV). Most commentaries agree that God's idea of being fruitful applies not only to reproduction in terms of producing children but also from a spiritual standpoint in terms of helping others to find Christ as their personal Lord and Savior.

Spiritual reproduction also could apply to individuals bearing fruit for the Lord, "love, joy, peace, longsuffering, gentleness, goodness, faith, meekness, and temperance" (Gal. 5:22–23). Thus God wants each believer to be a "creative, fruitful, and reproductive individual" (Robertson, 1984).

In addition to physical and spiritual reproduction, God desires human beings to have dominion over Satan. This is possible for believers since Jesus gave them authority over Satan, or the devil. To do this a believer has to request authority in the name of Jesus. The Bible encourages believers to "resist the devil, and he will flee from you" (James 4:7). God wants human beings to take dominion over the earth as well. This realm of dominion covers such things as the birds, the animals, and the fields. God wants human beings to be good stewards of His creation.

The main purpose of man here on earth is to glorify God, love Him, and serve Him forever. Jesus gave human beings two great commandments, the first being, "Thou shalt love the Lord thy God with all thy heart, and with all thy soul, and with all thy mind. And the second is like unto it, Thou shalt love thy neighbour as thyself" (Matt. 22:37, 39). God desires that all human beings walk with Him, obey Him, surrender all to Him, and have fellowship with Him. The prophet Micah states this edict well: "He hath shewed thee, O man, what is good; and what doth the LORD require of thee, but to do justly, and to love mercy, and to walk humbly with thy God" (Mic. 6:8).

Many individuals have also asked about man's final destiny. The answer to this question depends on the beliefs that each individual holds at the time of his death. Those who are believers (born again in the spirit, or saved) will receive the gift of eternal life and be in the presence of God for eternity. All nonbelievers (unsaved people) will receive judgment, or eternal punishment, suffering, and sorrow, and be separated from God for eternity.

Sin

Many individuals have also questioned the meaning of sin. According to the Bible, sin is "falling short of the glory of God." In other words, it means *to miss the target or the mark*. God has established holy standards for human beings which He expects them to follow. Sin is what results when human beings fail to live up to such holy standards. Unrepentant sin results in separation from God.

The sins committed by human beings separate us from God in a spiritual sense. By committing sin, individuals either choose to do what God does not want them to do or they choose not to do what He wants them to do. To commit sin is nothing short of outright rebellion against God. It generally comes about due to the problem of selfishness or self-centeredness. The apostle Paul states that "whatsoever is not of faith is sin" (Rom. 14:23).

The Bible states, "For all have sinned, and come short of the glory of God" (Rom. 3:23). The Prophet Isaiah also stated that, "But your iniquities have separated between you and your God, and your sins have hid his face from you, that he will not hear" (Isa. 59:2). The appropriate response is to repent or turn away from sin and from being selfish or self-centered.

When individuals alienate themselves from God they are choosing to be separated from Him. Thus, their sins will not be forgiven. But when individuals ask God to forgive their sins, He will do so, and then these individuals can have a personal relationship with Him. One of the many reasons God created human beings is so they could have personal fellowship with Him.

Salvation

An individual cannot attain salvation by way of his own merit. It is a gift of God. Thus salvation cannot be earned by good works (as is believed to be the case in Hinduism) but it is based entirely on God's grace. The Bible states, "For by grace are ye saved through faith; and that not of yourselves: it is the gift of God: not of works, lest any man should boast" (Eph. 2:8–9). In order to receive the gift of salvation an individual has to accept Jesus Christ as his Savior by faith.

R.C. Sproul states, "Salvation is threefold: God in the past delivered us from the penalty of sin (Romans 8:1–4); God in the present delivers us from the power of sin (Romans 8:13); and God in the future will deliver us from the presence of sin (Romans 13:11)." Sproul emphasizes that salvation must be received by faith.

God loved human beings so much that He sent His only begotten Son (Jesus) to come to earth in human form and sacrifice His life to pay the penalty for man's sins. The Bible states, "For God so loved the world, that he gave his only begotten Son, that whosoever believeth in him should not perish, but have everlasting life" (John3:16). The Bible also states, "Who his own self bare our sins in his own body on the tree, that we, being dead to sins, should live unto righteousness: by whose stripes ye were healed" (1 Peter 2:24).

In addition, the Bible states that "Neither is there salvation in any other: for there is none other name under heaven given among men, whereby we must be saved" (Acts 4:12). The Scripture that most touched my heart when I was seeking the truth as it related to God was spoken by Jesus and states, "I am the way, the truth, and the life: no man cometh unto the Father, but by me" (John 14:6). Thus, I came to a realization that Hindu deities or gods cannot save and none of them died to pay the penalty for my sin.

When Jesus died, He took all the sins committed by humanity upon Himself and paid the price for all of their sins by sacrificing His own body and blood. He died as a sacrifice to cover all the sins of the world. All individuals need to do is admit that they are sinners in need of salvation, ask Christ to forgive their sins, and then to accept Him by faith as their personal Lord and Savior. All that it takes to do this is described in the Bible, "That if thou shalt confess with thy mouth the Lord Jesus, and shalt believe in thine heart that God hath raised him from the dead, thou shalt be saved" (Rom. 10:9).

The apostle Paul states that, "God commendeth his love toward us, in that, while we were yet sinners, Christ died for us" (Rom. 5:8). He furthermore adds clarification when he states, "For whosoever shall call upon the name of the Lord shall be saved" (Rom. 10:13).

The Afterlife

Someday God will judge every individual, believers as well as non-believers. Every individual will someday stand before the judgment seat of Christ. At this time all persons will either receive or forfeit rewards based on how they lived and in accordance with what and in whom they believed. The Bible states,

> For whether we live, we live unto the Lord; and whether we die, we die unto the Lord: whether we live therefore, or die, we are the Lord's. For to this end Christ both died, and rose, and revived, that He might be Lord both of the dead and the living. But why dost thou judge thy brother? or why dost thou set at nought thy brother? for we shall all stand before the judgment seat of Christ.
>
> —Rom. 14:8–10

The Bible states that all unbelievers will face the great white throne of judgment (Rev. 20:11–5). All those who believe in Christ will spend eternity in heaven and in the presence of the Lord. The book of Revelation also clarifies that all those who do not put their faith or trust in Jesus will suffer in hell for all of eternity (Rev. 20:14–15).

Whether or not an individual should receive the gift of salvation is the single most important decision that any individual will ever make. This decision involves eternal consequences affecting the matter of life (heaven) or death (hell) for each person.

The Rapture

The term "rapture," although not specifically found in the Bible, literally means *caught up*. The English phrase "caught up" is translated from the Greek word "harpazo," which means *to seize upon with force* or *to snatch up*. This event is believed to be the time in which Jesus Christ appears in the clouds to catch up all believers to live with Him forever.

The Bible states,

> For the Lord himself shall descend from heaven with a shout, with the voice of the archangel, and with the trump of God: and the dead in Christ shall rise first: Then we which are alive and remain shall be caught up together with them in the clouds, to meet the Lord in the air: and so shall we ever be with the Lord. Wherefore comfort one another with these words.
> —1 Thess. 4:16–18

Many theologians have differing thoughts on just when the rapture may take place; however, many believers believe that this event is very near. When Jesus was asked by his disciples when this event was to take place, He replied that "no man knows the day or the hour" (Matt. 24:36). Since He did not say that believers would not know the month or the year, some have speculated that it may take place in September or October since this is the time of the "Feast of Firstfruits" and the "Feast of Trumpets."

When the disciples asked Jesus how they would know when the end of this age was at hand and the time of His coming was near, He stated, "Take heed that no man deceive you" (Matt. 24:4). The key word here is deception, since the time of the great tribulation as described by the prophet Joel is the time when there will be a great leader who will deceive almost the whole world. Furthermore, this deceiver (the anti-Christ) will force all to receive a mark on their forehead or hand in order to be able to buy or sell. According to the Scriptures, the souls of individuals who receive this mark will be condemned to hell for eternity.

I believe that the rapture will take place sometime before the great tribulation since the tribulation is a time of beginning judgment for all unbelievers. Jesus stated that in the last days it is going to be like it was in the days of Noah before the flood. In those days, they were eating, drinking, marrying, and giving in marriage, right up to the day that Noah entered the ark (See Matt. 24:37–38).

In the days of Noah, just before God's judgment fell on the unrighteous, God warned Noah of the coming flood since he and his family were seen to be the only righteous persons alive at that time. Christians are righteous because of their acceptance of Christ. In a manner similar to that of Noah, I believe that God will take Christians out of the world by rapture before the great tribulation, or coming judgment of God.

The Conclusion

Based on the material that I have presented from the Word of God (the Bible), it is evident that Jesus died for our sins. Furthermore, the Bible clearly states that He is the only one (God-Man) who is able to save mankind from their sins. Thus, He is the only one who can bless individuals with eternal life. When an individual chooses to accept Jesus Christ as his personal Lord and Savior and to follow after Him, he is putting himself in the right position as a child of God to receive all the many spiritual blessings that come along with salvation. These blessings for believers include, but are not limited to, the following:

1. They do not have to face any more condemnation (Rom.8:1).
2. They can look forward to serving the true God (Matt. 22:37).
3. They can rest be assured that they have received the truth (John 14:6).
4. They can be thankful that Jesus made them a new creature (2 Cor. 5:17–18).

5. They can be thankful that He saved them by His grace and not on their works (Eph. 2:8–9).

6. They can be thankful that Jesus gave them eternal life that He promised and provided for them (1 John 5:11; 2 Tim. 1:1).

7. They can be thankful that they can look forward to His appearing (Titus 2:13).

Individuals cannot ignore or minimize the teachings of Jesus, His crucifixion or His physical resurrection. The evidence of His coming to earth to pay the penalty for the sin of mankind is so strong that no individual can deny or reject this truth. The resurrection of Jesus Christ is the one aspect that sets Christianity apart from other religions and cults. "It is the objective evidence for this confirming miracle that sets Christianity apart from the other religions in a dramatic way" (Bickel & Jantz, 2002). Furthermore, Christianity is a religion that can truly be tested.

A Final Note

If Jesus is the only way to eternal life and heaven, then why do so few people accept this free gift of salvation? In the Bible, Jesus predicted that only a very small number of people would choose to be saved, "Because strait is the gate, and narrow is the way, which leadeth unto life, and few there be that find it" (Matt. 7:14).

The God of the Bible gives all individuals a free will. He does not force anyone to accept Him. Jesus desires that each individual choose salvation based on his or her own free will. The Bible states that "And ye shall seek me, and find me, when ye shall search for me with all your heart" (Jer. 29:13). But, since the beginning of time, human beings have been rebellious, selfish, and self-centered. They have been known to carry this self-centeredness to such an extent that, rather than admitting they are in need of a savior, they come up with all kinds of excuses for not wanting to follow the truth as it relates to God, especially when it pertains to Jesus. Some of these excuses include, but are not limited to, the following:

1. Putting salvation on hold due to more concern for the cares of this life, that is, wanting to live in the present and in the now and not wanting to worry about the future.
2. Rejecting the gift of eternal life mostly due to pride and self-righteousness. Some individuals are doubtful as to how Jesus' death that took place 2,000 years ago can affect an individual's life in the present.
3. Believing that God will let those individuals into heaven who have lived a good life and have not intentionally hurt or harmed anyone.
4. Some individuals, preferring to wait, do not want to be rushed into anything because they believe that, "I am in good health and might live a long life; there is no need to rush the decision right now. Whatever it is, it can wait until I am ready."
5. Then there are those individuals who disagree with the Word of God. They might not agree to the fact that Jesus Christ is unique and different from all others.

There may be many other reasons why an individual would choose to reject or deny the truth about Jesus and His offer of salvation. Although it is true that all individuals are given a free will, every person needs to face up to the realization that every choice and decision comes with its own consequence(s). Thus, it is important for individuals to objectively look at everything by examining the evidence from every possible viewpoint and then be open to accept the truth convincingly without any doubt or reservation.

SECTION FIVE

OTHER MAJOR
WORLD RELIGIONS

CHAPTER 24

THE TEACHINGS OF BUDDHISM

THIS BOOK PRESENTS information on the four largest religions in the world, including Buddhism, Christianity, Islam, and Hinduism. These three religions put together represent about 80 percent of the world's population.

Facts & Statistics

Buddhism is the fourth largest religion in the world, with more than 400 million people who have adopted it as their religion. It is superseded in number only by Christianity, Islam, and Hinduism. Buddhism originated in India (modern day Nepal) and eventually spread to China, Japan, Korea, Tibet, and other oriental countries, including the Philippines, Thailand, and Vietnam. Later on, Buddhism spread to other parts of the world such as North America and Europe.

Founder & Origins

Buddha, also known as the "enlightened one," is credited as being the founder of Buddhism. He was given the name of Gautama Siddhartha at the time of his birth around (560-480 B.C.). Many Hindus strongly believe that Buddha was actually Lord Vishnu while he was in his 9th incarnation. Buddha was born into a Hindu family who resided in Northeastern India (modern-day Nepal) and belonged to the Kshatriya caste.

Siddhartha, another birth name for Buddha, was born to King Suddhodana and Queen Mahamaya from the tribe of Shakya. Buddha is also referred to as "Shakyamuni." The name Siddhartha means *wish fulfilled* and Shakyamuni means *sage* of the Shakya tribe. Siddhartha's mother died when he was only seven days old, and his aunt from his mother's side raised him. He married his cousin, Princess Yasodhara, also known as "keeper of radiance," when he was just sixteen.

A Short History

The "Tripitaka," which means *three baskets of the law*, is the sacred text of Buddhism. It comprises a three-volume collection that includes all of Buddha's teachings, as well as several other Sutras (discourses). Buddhism teaches that the nature of God is difficult to define. On one hand, some Buddhists consider themselves godless (atheistic), while others identify themselves as being either animistic or polytheistic, meaning that they worship various deities and even celestial beings. Buddha encouraged his followers to keep to his teachings "Dharma" and discouraged them from worshipping any god.

Buddhists from the East tend to view Jesus as an avatar but not as God, whereas Buddhists from the West tend to view him as a great enlightened teacher. Buddhists also believe that men do not possess an immortal soul. Author Ron Rhodes states that human nature consists of "five temporarily connected aggregates: material form (rupa), feeling (vedana), perception (sanna), dispositions (sankhara), and consciousness (vinnana)." Buddha taught that all creatures, including humans, are fictional, and thus the concept of self is nonexistent.

Buddhists also believe in reincarnation. In this sense their beliefs are very similar to that of Hinduism. How does an individual attain salvation? Buddhism teaches that ignorance rather than sin is what keeps an individual from attaining salvation. According to Buddhism, salvation is attained by following the eightfold path. In order to follow this path, an individual must perform specific actions while at the same time keeping his attitudes in check with those specified by the teachings of Buddha.

When individuals follow the eightfold path they become liberated from the cycle of reincarnation (samsara). The goal of Buddhism is for individuals to attain Nirvana (the third Noble Truth) and thereby eliminate their desires or cravings so that they can escape suffering. The meaning of Nirvana is a *blowing out* that is likened to the quenching or extinguishing of a candle flame.

Several key figures are described in the teachings of Buddha. Ashoka was an Indian emperor who lived from 273 to 232 B.C. He was known for spreading Buddhism by sending out missionaries. Nagarjuna, the most influential Buddhist who ever lived, was an Indian philosopher who lived from A.D. 150 to 250. Dalai Lama the 14th was known for winning the Nobel Peace Prize in 1989 and for being the spiritual leader of Tibetan Buddhism. Buddhists are currently anticipating the arrival of Lord Maitreya, or the future Buddha.

Many individuals are attracted to the teachings of Buddhism, but perhaps for all the wrong reasons. This religion allows individuals to attain morality through a do-it-yourself process. Thus this religion does not recognize a personal God and dismisses the need for an individual to assume accountability. This means an *accountability to God*. For instance, Christians give an account to God on judgment day. Budhists, on the other hand, may not have to give any account to their god.

Furthermore, this religion does not embrace the existence of almighty God. Thus it does not recognize sin or the need for atonement. In addition, this religion does not recognize an ultimate reality since everything is constantly changing. Buddhism further teaches that the primary problem in an individual's life is suffering, which is thought to be brought about by a desire for worldly things.

Buddha is considered to be a title rather than a name. At the time of Prince Siddhartha's birth, a Brahmin priest predicted that he would someday rule over the land. The priest suggested that the prince be kept from experiencing the reality of death and decay in order to bring about this prediction. The priest believed that if the prince were exposed to death and decay then he would strive to become a great saint or ascetic. The priest probably said this from a philosophical view point, meaning, the more one is exposed to life's problems and circumstances, the more one can become inquisitive and hence seek and find solutions to the problems that may arise.

CHAPTER 25

CENTRAL BELIEFS OF BUDDHISM

FOR THE MOST part, Buddhism is considered to be a godless or somewhat atheistic religion. Although "Buddha acknowledged the existence of impermanent gods, he discouraged their worship" (Rhodes, 2007). But not all those who practice Buddhism are atheistic. Some consider themselves to be either animistic or polytheistic.

Buddhists believe that knowing God is irrelevant. They further believe that a pursuit of knowing God can even interfere with an individual's quest for enlightenment. Buddha encouraged his disciples to follow his teachings, probably more so than any other religious teachings. Even though Buddha never denied the existence of God, he did not believe in Him.

Buddhists believe that Buddhism is more a way of life rather than a religion. Furthermore, Buddha did not suppose himself to be deity. Rather, he used himself instead of God as an example to humanity. He encouraged his disciples to share his teachings to others and not to keep any information on his teachings to themselves.

Jesus

Buddhists do not consider Jesus as being a part of their perspective of the world. The Buddhists from the East ignore Jesus, as well as His deity. Although some Buddhists in Asia may consider Jesus to be an avatar (incarnation), they do not believe that He is God. Buddhists from the West consider Jesus to be an enlightened teacher.

Sacred Texts

Tripitaka is the main text of Buddhism. It is a three-volume collection that is much larger than the Christian Bible and comprises all of Buddha's teachings. There are several other sacred Buddhist writings such as the Mahavastu (Great Story), the Jataka tales, and numerous other Sutras (discourses). The Mahavastu relates the story of Buddha's life and the Jataka tales relate about 550 stories on Buddha's former lives. These writings describe the life and sayings of Buddha. They were written approximately 500 years after the death of Buddha. The three main collections of the Tripitaka are described below.

1. Abidharma pitaka (basket of scholasticism) comprises philosophical doctrines.
2. Sutra pitaka (basket of threads) comprises the stories and teachings of Buddha.
3. Vinaya pitaka (basket of discipline) comprises laws and regulations for monks and nuns.

The Sects or Divisions

Buddhism consists of at least four different divisions or sects. But only two of these divisions (Theravada and Mahayana) are considered to be primary and original. Theravada is also known as Hinayana. The Theravada sect consists of conservative Buddhists, whereas the Mahayana sect consists of more liberal Buddhists. The conservative and the liberal Buddhists do not see eye to eye on many important issues. The texts for these divisions were written about 400 years after the death of Buddha.

Mahayana is defined as Greater Vehicle and Hinayana is defined as Lesser Vehicle. The school of Zen is derived from Mahayana Buddhism. Author Ron Rhodes explains,

> Theravada Buddhism teaches that Buddhism is for a select few (full-time monks), and that Buddha was just a man—an ethical teacher.

> Mahayana Buddhism teaches that Buddhism is for all people and that Buddha was just a man. Mahayana Buddhism teaches that Buddha is for all the people and that the Buddha was a manifestation of the Universal Absolute (and thus, was a divine person).
> —Rhodes 2007

Buddhism teaches that humans do not possess an immaterial soul, that is, an unchanging soul. Rather, they have five components or aggregates: physical body (rupa), feelings (vedana), ideas (sanna), dispositions (sankhara), and consciousness (vinnana).

Sin

Buddhism teaches that sin is related to desire or attachment. It also teaches that ignorance, rather than sin, is what blocks the way to salvation. The concept of sin can be described by the four Noble Truths: 1) All life is full of pain and suffering, 2) the root cause of pain and suffering is desire or attachment, 3) suffering can be rid of by eliminating the desires, and 4) to get rid of these cravings one must follow the eightfold path.

Salvation

An individual can attain salvation by following the eightfold path. By following this path a soul can be liberated from the cycle of reincarnation (samara) and eventually be absorbed into the universal absolute. Buddhism believes that an individual attains salvation by reaching a state of Nirvana. It also believes that once individuals attain Nirvana they can eliminate suffering and rebirth by getting rid of all desire.

Afterlife

Buddhism teaches that at death "a person's five aggregates (or components) are dismantled and cease to be a cohesive unit. Through reincarnation, one's desires or feelings wander across to another body and one then lives another life, making further progress toward absorption into the Absolute" (Rhodes, 2007). Thus Buddhism does not believe in the existence of heaven or hell. It further teaches that either individuals are reborn to suffer more (through samsara, or endless wandering) or they reach the state of Nirvana (the end of all suffering).

Four Noble Truths

The young prince's father showered him with much love and affection and also supplied him with all of his necessities, as well as all of the luxuries of life. In an effort to make sure that his son's life was happy, the king provided his son with riches and comfort. But the prince was ignorant as to what life was like outside the palace walls since he had never before left the palace. One day the young prince asked his father if he could venture out into the real world on his own so that he could explore and experience the outside world for himself.

The king granted his son's wish, and the young prince left with his charioteer one day to see firsthand what life was like outside the confines of the palace. The charioteer and the young prince set out on one trip each day for a total of four trips. What he saw during these trips completely changed his way of thinking for life.

During his first trip he saw an elderly man who was ill. His charioteer told him that everyone eventually gets old and grows weary. During his second trip he saw a man who was very sick and was lying on the ground, shaking and shivering. His charioteer explained that people have been known to get ill. During his third trip he was shocked to have seen a dead body. His charioteer told him that everyone has to die someday. Witnessing the corpse made such a dramatic impact on him that he began to meditate.

During his fourth and final trip the young prince saw an old man with a shaven head who was wearing a yellow robe. This man was acting very serene, calm, and appeared to be very much at peace with himself. The charioteer told the prince that this old man was a holy man (an ascetic) who had attained both enlightenment and complete freedom. Being moved by the appearance of this holy man, he wanted to personally experience this enlightenment.

Siddhartha, who was married and had a son of his own by the name of Rahula (fetter or bond or chain), was about twenty-nine years old at the time of these trips. He was thought to have probably been torn inside since on the one hand his wife had just given birth to their son and yet he was making plans to renounce everything (the palace, the kingship, the luxuries, the servants, married life, and parenthood) in order to experience enlightenment.

Although he had made up his mind to leave the palace at any cost, he did not want to do it openly and publicly since he did not want to hurt anyone, especially his wife. Thus, he waited until everyone in the palace went to sleep. He then saddled up his horse and left in the middle of the night. He visited a place called Gotama where there were many centers of spiritual learning and, thus, began his personal mission to find answers to questions that he had about life, suffering, death, and enlightenment.

Gautama is believed to have spent about six years meditating under a bodhi tree, which is located near the famous Ganges River, a place where the four "Noble Truths" came to him. These four Noble Truths are as follows:

1. All life is suffering (Dukha)
2. Suffering stems from desires or attachment (Trishna)
3. There can be an end to desire, which means an end to suffering (Nirvana)
4. Desires can be eliminated by following the eightfold path (Maggha)

The Eightfold Path

A way of life that is known as the eightfold path aims to avoid any extremes of pleasure (on one end) and self-denial (on the other end) and involves both attitudes and actions. The eightfold path is as follows:

1. Right view or understanding
2. Right purpose or resolve or intention or aspirations
3. Right speech
4. Right conduct or action
5. Right livelihood
6. Right effort
7. Right alertness or mindfulness
8. Right concentration or meditation or contemplative absorption

The eightfold path is divided into three categories: wisdom, ethics, and meditation. The first two paths are categorized under wisdom, paths three, four, and five are categorized under the ethics, and paths six, seven, and eight are categorized under the meditation category.

Three Jewels

Three jewels are referred to in Buddhism. Author Len Woods describes these as follows:

1. "Buddha is known as the Awakened One and is the one who discovered the way to enlightenment.
2. Dharma is defined as the teachings of Buddha on what is true and all that they pertain to.
3. Sangha is defined as the Spiritual Community that embraces, practices, and promotes the teachings of Buddha." (Woods, 2008).

Ten Precepts

There are ten precepts that Buddhism endorses. The first five apply to all Buddhists; all ten of these precepts apply to the monks as follows:

1. No killing of living things
2. No stealing
3. No lying
4. No intoxicants
5. No sexual abuse or unchastity
6. No inappropriate eating
7. No attending or participation in singing, dancing, musicals, or dramatic performances
8. No decorative accessories
9. No luxurious furnishings or bedding
10. No possession of silver and gold

CHAPTER 26

CHRISTIANITY COMPARED WITH BUDDHISM

BUDDHA NEVER CLAIMED to be divine, nor did he teach anything about God. Rather, he taught about how to eliminate suffering through human effort, or by works. The original Buddhism (also known as Theravada) did not encourage the practice of faith, worship, prayer, praise, or forgiveness of sins. Buddhism is a religion that does not recognize the existence of God (for conservatives) and, thus, it does not teach anything about God.

Christianity's Biblical Response

Christianity recognizes the existence of God. His existence is evident in all of His creation, the universe, as well as the human race. The Bible states, "The heavens declare the glory of God; and the firmament showeth his handiwork" (Ps. 19:1). One of the main purposes of religion is that man might have a relationship with God, and the Bible confirms this by declaring that the whole duty of man is to fear God and keep His commands (see Ecclesiastes 12:13).

Prophecy and Miracles

Buddha did not perform any miracles, nor did he give any prophecies.

Christianity's Biblical Response

As recorded in the Bible, Jesus spoke prophetically and performed many miracles.

Suffering and Love

In Buddhism, a person is motivated to escape suffering. Furthermore, it teaches that love is just one element among others, such as hope, joy, and peace. According to Buddhists, the concept of suffering focuses on the four Noble Truths. Thus they believe that man suffers due to his desire for attachment to things of this world, such as personal enjoyment and material possessions. Furthermore, Buddhism does not provide a solid solution to suffering other than depending on human effort.

Christianity's Biblical Response

In Christianity, a person is motivated to love God as well as others. Indeed, the two greatest commandments that Jesus taught in the Bible state, "Jesus said unto him, Thou shalt love the Lord thy God with all thy heart, and with all thy soul, and with all thy mind....Thou shalt love thy neighbour as thyself" (Matt. 22:37, 39). Accordingly, Christianity places a strong emphasis on love, not only towards God but also towards others. "And now abide faith, hope, love, but the greatest of these is love (1 Cor. 13:13, NKJV).

The Bible agrees that suffering is part of life as it states, "Yet man is born unto trouble, as the sparks fly upward" (Job 5:7). The Bible also states that the existence of suffering is due to man's sin or temptation to sin. It further states that the way to overcome desires and suffering is not to try to conquer it in our own strength (that is, by works) but to trust in God for the victory over it. The Bible states, "God is our refuge and strength, a very present help in time of trouble" (Ps. 46:1). The Bible provides a genuine solution to suffering. All individuals have to do is to trust God.

Humanity

The attainment of enlightenment by individuals is the primary focus in Buddhism. Buddhism teaches that human beings have only a temporary existence and are not worth much. Furthermore, Buddhism may hold the perspective that a man's body is a hindrance.

Buddhism believes in rebirth (reincarnation), Karma (action), and Nirvana (release from samsara). Accordingly, Buddhists believe that after individuals die, they return to earth to live as another human being and that this cycle of birth and rebirth continues until the individual is released, or attains Nirvana. Karma in Buddhism works in a similar manner to that of Hinduism. The present events are based on the past lives, and what happens in the future is determined by the current or present actions.

Christianity's Biblical Response

According to Christianity, an individual's primary focus is to serve God and others. Jesus said of Himself, "The Son of Man did not come to be served, but to serve" (Matt. 20:28, NKJV). Furthermore, the Bible states that human beings are created in the image of God and have infinite worth. It also states that human beings live forever. In accordance with Christianity, an individual is perceived as being an instrument for glorifying God. The Bible states, "Know ye not that your body is the temple of the Holy Ghost which is in you" (1 Cor. 6:19).

The Bible clearly states that "it is appointed for men to die once, but after this the judgment" (Heb. 9:27, NKJV). Furthermore, it states, "These shall go away into everlasting punishment, but the righteous into life eternal" (Matt. 25:31–46).

Sin

In Buddhism, human beings do not sin against a Supreme Being.

Christianity's Biblical Response

According to Christianity, the Bible states that "all have sinned and come short of the glory of God" (Rom, 3:23). Furthermore, the Bible confirms an individual's sin against a Holy God, "Against thee, thee only, have I sinned, and done this evil in thy sight" (Ps. 51:4). The sins of human beings are committed against God even though they may affect not only the person committing the sin but others as well.

Salvation

Buddhism teaches that the only way for individuals to attain salvation (or reach a state of Nirvana) is by following the eightfold path; each individual is, working out their own salvation. By following this path, they believe that they may escape the endless series of rebirths (reincarnation) and eventually attain Nirvana.

Buddhists disagree on the ways that individuals can attain salvation. For example, conservative Buddhists, those belonging to the Theravada sect, believe in following the eightfold path in order to attain Nirvana. Liberal Buddhists believe that there are many different ways by which an individual can accomplish the same purpose in life (referring to salvation).). Author David Pratte indicates that Buddhists believe many lifetimes are required to realize perfection. One must pass through 4 stages in which 10 hindrances are overcome. Each stage may take many lives. Gautama took at least 550 lives to realize perfection (Pratte, 2008). Thus this process is very dependent on human effort.

Christianity's Biblical Response

According to Christianity, salvation is entirely based on grace and not works. An individual attains salvation by trusting in Jesus Christ as one's Lord and Savior. The Bible clearly states that human beings cannot save themselves without God. The Bible states, "The wages of sin is death" (Rom. 6:23), and unless individuals ask God for His forgiveness, there is nothing they can do to save themselves.

Afterlife

Buddhism believes in repeated reincarnations until an individual attains Nirvana.

Christianity's Biblical Response

According to Christianity, human beings will enter either heaven or hell based on their state of salvation at the time of their death.

Resurrection

When Buddha died, his physical body was cremated but there was no resurrection.

Christianity's Biblical Response

When Jesus was crucified, He was resurrected to life again, and there is enough evidence available to prove that this really happened.

The Conclusion

The particular sect of Buddhism (Theravada or Mahayana) determines whether or not its followers worship either false gods or no god. Buddhism encourages its followers to work out by human efforts the solution to their problems over a period of many lives. Even more confusing is the issue that Buddhism takes on many forms (beliefs). There are a wide variety of beliefs among the different sects which often sound contradictory.

Author John Noss notes that,

The rather odd fact is that there ultimately developed within Buddhism so many forms of religious organizations, cults, beliefs, such great changes even in the fundamentals of the faith, that one must say Buddhism as a whole is really like Hinduism, a family of religions rather than a single religion.

—Noss, 1969

A Final Note

Although Buddhism and Christianity differ on many life issues, the most fundamental one is that of how they recognize Jesus versus Buddha. The Christian apologist Patrick Zukeran states, "After a comparative study, I came to realize Buddha was a great teacher who lived a noble life, but Christ is the unique revelation of God who is to be worshipped as our eternal Lord and Savior" (Zukeran, 2008).

The Bible clearly states in all four Gospels that the facts provided about God and Jesus are true. It also provides instructions on how human beings should worship the only true God. It further explains in detail the process whereby a human being can receive forgiveness of sin from Jesus, the One who paid the penalty for the sin of all mankind. All human beings need to do is to trust in and obey Jesus, ask Him for forgiveness of their sins, ask Him to come into their hearts and receive Him as their Lord and Savior. Then He gives them the free gift of eternal life.

CHAPTER 27

THE TEACHINGS AND CENTRAL BELIEFS OF ISLAM

A LTHOUGH ISLAM IS the youngest of the main world religions, it is the fastest growing religion in the world and is second only to Christianity in number of adherents. Two Christian authors state the following about Islam: "It is growing by about 68,000 people every 24 hours, and expanding rapidly in the United States" (Ankerberg & Burroughs, 2008).

Approximately one billion, or one out of every six persons in the world today, is a Muslim (follower of Islam). Of these, approximately seven million have made the United States their home. The first mosque or place of worship for Muslims in the United States was built in Cedar Rapids, Iowa, in 1934.

Founder and Origins

Muhammad is considered to be the founder of Islam. He was born into an aristocratic family in A.D. 570. His birth name was Muhammad Bin Abdullah, and Mecca (located in modern-day Saudi Arabia) was the city of his birth. He was raised by his grandfather, a Bedouin tribesman. His father died before his birth. His mother died when he was only six years old. Muhammad's grandfather died shortly thereafter and he moved in with his uncle who was the head of the Quaraish clan or tribe.

Muhammad was a shepherd who could neither read nor write. But since he had a knack for commerce, he was a very successful merchant. Author Len Woods notes that "Muslims do not consider him to be divine, nor is he regarded as a savior. He is believed to be God's final messenger and prophet" (Woods, 2008). Islam teaches that the God of Muhammad is Allah, which means *the God.*

Muhammad was about twenty-five when he married Khadija, a wealthy forty year old widow who was the owner of the caravan business that he was managing. They made Mecca their hometown due to its economic importance and its popularity as a resting place for caravan traders. The couple had six children, two sons and four daughters. Fatima was the best known of all his children. She later married Muhammad's cousin, Ali, who was regarded to be the divinely ordained successor of Muhammad.

Mecca is also the location for the Ka'bah, a black cubic-shaped structure. According to Muslims, Abraham of the Old Testament placed this black stone in Mecca. At the time of Muhammad, the Ka'bah housed about 360 deities, of which a man of god is the prominent one.

According to one author, "Each Arabian tribe had hand-picked its own deity and came to Mecca each year to pay homage to its god" (Halverson, 2003). Supposedly, it was during one of these pilgrimages to Mecca that Muhammad came to believe in only one god whom he called "Allah."

A Short History

Islam is a monotheistic religion, as it believes in worshipping just one god. The word Islam means *submission and peace.* Islam came into existence around the 7th century A.D. According to Islam, Muhammad was the descendent of a long line of great prophets, which included Adam, Abraham, Moses, and Jesus. Muslims believe that there is no need for any other prophets, as Muhammad was the last one.

The word Muslim means *those who submit*. Islam commands its followers to completely surrender their will and obedience to Allah. The two most important tenets of Islam are its beliefs in "The Five Doctrines of Islam" and the obligations otherwise known as "The Five Pillars of Islam." Muslim believers claim that Islam is a unique religion that supersedes all other religions.

For Muslim believers, the message of Islam is far more important than its founder, Muhammad. In fact, Muslims find it offensive to be called Mohammedans, as this carries the connotation of worshiping Muhammad. To Muslims, Islam is more than a religion; it is a way of life that allows them to practice and follow a way of peace, mercy, and forgiveness.

When Muhammad was forty years old (during the year 610), he spent a lot of time in a nearby cave. He received his first revelation (series of mystical visions) while there. According to Muslims, these visions not only changed Muhammad's life but also the world thereafter. He supposedly received several revelations or visions from the angel Gabriel.

Eventually he compiled all these revelations into the sacred scripture, or texts, otherwise referred to as the "Qur'an," which means *to recite*, or *that which is to be read*. The Qur'an is divided into 114 chapters. Its size is equivalent in length to about four-fifths of the size of the New Testament of the Bible.

Muslims believe that at first Muhammad was skeptical as to whether these visions came from God or from demonic spirits. But his wife convinced him that the visions did indeed come from God. Later on she became his first convert. Eventually he believed that God delivered these visions to him through the archangel Gabriel. The main theme of this message was that there was only one true god (Allah) and that idolatry was an abomination.

Two years after receiving his first vision, Muhammad began to preach and enlist new converts. He continued to receive more visions and revelations, and during this time Muslims believed that the angel Gabriel told Muhammad to recite. He refused to do so three times but the angel insisted he "recite in the name of thy God (Allah) who created." He finally gave in to this command. But since he could neither read nor write, he recited all these visions to his followers who recorded them on his behalf.

Around the time of these recordings, there was political expansion and a lot of turbulence from both a political and military standpoint. Thus Muhammad and his followers met with a lot of opposition not only from political and military unrest but also from a religious perspective. For example, many people in Mecca were hostile to his teachings since they did not want to hear about a holy and moral god. Because of this hostility he began to make enemies.

In order to escape this persecution, Muhammad and his followers decided to migrate to the north to a city known as Medina, or "the city of the prophet," in A.D. 622. It was while he was in Medina that people began to accept him and his teachings. Thus the first Islamic community was founded in this city.

Christian authors Ankerberg and Burroughs note that "all Islamic calendars mark this date, July 16, 622, as their beginning. So, for example, A.D. 630 corresponds to 8 AH (in the year of the hijira)" (Ankerberg and Burroughs, 2008). The term "hijira" means *flight or to flee*. Muhammad and his followers "fled" from Mecca to Medina.

God

Islam teaches that Allah is the only true god. Furthermore, Allah has absolute unity in himself. Thus he does not have a son or partner, as is the case with the Trinity in Christianity. The greatest sin according to Islam beliefs is "shrik," which means *to associate something or anything with God*. Thus Muslims believe that Christians are guilty of "shrik" since they believe in the Trinity. They also believe that since fatherhood is a human concept, it cannot be associated with God.

Allah is believed to be transcendent. Furthermore, Allah is perceived to be more closely related with judgment, as opposed to grace, mercy, or power (Suras-6:142; & 7:31). In addition, Allah should not be viewed as the Father (Suras-19:88–92; & 112:3). Muslims view Allah as a divinity that is all hearing, all knowing, all-powerful, all seeking, and all willing. The Justice of Allah is the most important value that Muslims possess.

Muhammad

Muhammad is believed to be a true prophet of God and considered to be God's last prophet. His teachings are considered as being perfect and without error.

Many Muslims believe that Muhammad was referred to in the Bible on at least three different instances. For example, the 18th chapter of Deuteronomy refers to "God raising a prophet." Muslims believe that Muhammad was the prophet being referred to in this verse. Another example that Muslims point to is the "mighty one coming with a sword" (Ps 45:3–5). According to Muslims, Muhammad is known as the "prophet of the sword." Muslims believe that this verse could not be applied to Jesus since Jesus never came with a sword. A third example that Muslims refer to is "Muslims argue that the 'comforter' referred to in John 14:16; 15:26; and 16:7 is Muhammad. They note that the Qur'an refers to Muhammad as Allah's 'praised one' (Sura-61:6)" (Rhodes, 2000). But in the Holy Bible, Jesus is referring to the comforter as being the Holy Spirit.

Jesus Christ

Muslims believe that Jesus was born of the Virgin Mary. They also believe that Jesus was a revered prophet but that He was a lesser prophet than Muhammad. Although they believe that Jesus performed genuine miracles, they do not see Him as being God or having a divine nature. Moreover, they do not believe that Jesus was crucified and died on the cross since Allah would not allow one of His own prophets to die such a death. Instead, they believe that He ascended directly into heaven without dying.

The Qur'an

Muslims believe that the Qur'an was revealed to Muhammad by the angel Gabriel. The Qur'an accepts the biblical Law of

Moses, Psalms of David, and the Gospel of Jesus. However, many Muslim scholars claim that the Jews and Christians have distorted the original and divine revelations of these Holy Scriptures. They further teach that the Qur'an is an absolute miracle since it has been free of any errors, alterations, or variations from its beginning.

The Qur'an is considered to be of God due to its beauty and eloquence, especially since Muhammad was an unlettered prophet; he could neither read nor write. Author Ron Rhodes adds, "The fact that the Qur'an shows remarkable affinity with modern science shows it is divine. The Qur'an is said to supersede all previous revelations" (Rhodes, 2000). Muslims believe the Qur'an is Allah's last and complete book. It is divided into 114 suras or chapters.

The Five Pillars

The five pillars form the basis for Islam and include: Shahadah, Salat, Zakat, Sawm, and Hajj. These pillars refer to the obligations, or tenets of faith, which every Muslim is required to follow in order to live a good and responsible life. They also serve as an anchor for Muslim life. Muslims are required to believe and apply these tenets to their daily life.

The first pillar represents a state of faith. The other four are believed to be major exercises of faith and can be performed daily, weekly, monthly, or annually. The last pillar of faith must be undertaken once in a lifetime. The following describes the five pillars of faith.

Pillar Number 1: Shahadah

The meaning of Shahadah is to bear witness. Muslims are expected to publicly recite this pillar. They are also expected to show their profession of faith by reciting the creed, which in Arabic reads as follows: "La Ilaha Illa Allah, Muhammadur Rasoolu Allah." When translated into English this creed reads as follows: "There is no God but Allah, and Muhammad is his prophet," or messenger. An individual confirms his faith in Islam by repeating this creed in Arabic throughout his lifetime.

Pillar Number 2: Salat

Since prayer demonstrates obedience to Allah, it is very important to Muslims. A Muslim is required to pray five times daily while facing Mecca: before sunrise, just after noon, later in the afternoon, before sunset, and after dark. A Muslim is allowed to pray while at home, at the mosque, or elsewhere. But on Fridays, Muslims must attend the mosque at noontime to pray together with other believers in order to support unity in their faith.

Pillar Number 3: Zakat

Zakat means *to purify*. A Zakat is a required tax that is paid to the state government once a year, and equals about 2.5 percent of a person's gross income. The money is donated to a Muslim community so as to benefit widows, orphans, the sick, and the travelers. It also involves such acts as giving alms for the poor and needy. These funds (alms) may also be used to build mosques or finance Muslim missionaries. Muslims believe that by giving these monies they free their soul from greed and gluttony.

Pillar Number 4: Sawm

The word Sawm means *fasting*. Muslims are required to fast during the month of Ramadan, or the ninth Muslim month. It is the same month that Muhammad was believed to have received the revelation of the Qur'an. Fasting during this time begins at daybreak and ends at sunset. During fasting Muslims are forbidden from any eating, drinking, smoking, and sexual intercourse. The practice of fasting is required by all Muslims, except for small children, the sick, the mentally ill, and the elderly. The main reason for fasting is to attain self-purification.

Pillar Number 5: Hajj

The word Hajj means *pilgrimage*. It is a journey that most Muslims dream about and highly anticipate. The reason for this journey is to honor the life of Muhammad. It also serves as a time for an individual to recommit or rededicate himself to Allah. Any individual who is physically healthy, financially able, and mentally sound is required to take this pilgrimage at least once in his lifetime. Each year, millions of Muslims make this journey to Mecca, usually in the twelfth month of the Islamic calendar year.

Five Doctrines or Articles of Faith

The Muslim creed consists of five articles, or doctrines of faith: belief in one god, angels, sacred scriptures, prophets, and the day of judgment. These five basic tenets or beliefs form the basis for all of the others. These are described in this section below.

Doctrine Number 1: God

There is only one god, known as Allah. The seven primary characteristics of Allah include: he has absolute unity (he cannot have any son or partner). He is all hearing, all knowing, all-powerful, all seeing, all speaking, and all willing. Allah is believed to be a personal god who is always close to each believer, as explained in the Qur'an: "God is nearer to man than his jugular vein" (Sura-50:16). Muslims use the words "Allah O Akbar," which means *God is great!*

Doctrine Number 2: Angels - (Jinn)

Muslims believe that there is a hierarchy of angels between Allah and humans. They also believe that angels are made of light energy and that they are capable of materializing in different forms. The Bible refers to some fallen angels, but Islam teaches that all angels serve Allah. Furthermore, Muslims believe that all human beings are assigned two angels that record all of their deeds, both good and bad. They further believe that these recorded deeds will be used to determine an individual's fate on the day of judgment.

Doctrine Number 3: Sacred Scriptures

Islam teaches that there are four inspired books: the Torah of Moses (Tawrat), the Psalms of David (Zabur), the Gospel of Jesus

Christ (Injil), and the Qur'an (the teachings of Muhammad). The Qur'an is God's complete and final revelation. Muslims believe that the Bible that Christians use today is distorted or inauthentic and full of errors.

Muslims believe that the Qur'an is Allah's final message to mankind, thus the Qur'an supersedes all previous existing revelations. Furthermore, Muslims strongly believe that the Qur'an is the only revelation that has been preserved in an uncorrupted state. Three of the most important themes in the Qur'an are: the oneness of Allah, Allah's messengers, and life after death.

Doctrine Number 4: Prophets

Islam accepts and recognizes the idea of prophets, just as Christianity and Judaism do, which makes Islam a prophetic religion. Muslims believe that Allah sent about 140,000 prophets throughout history. The Qur'an, however, mentions about 25 prophets, and these are considered of greater importance.

The Qur'an recognizes the following individuals as prophets sent by Allah: Adam, Abraham, Isaac, Ishmael, Jacob, Moses, Aaron, Joseph, Noah, Job, Elias, David, Solomon, Jonah, John the Baptist, Jesus, and Muhammad. Islam teaches that the message all the prophets gave was good for their time, but the message and teachings of Muhammad, they claim, are not only for all people but also for all the time.

Even though the Qur'an accepts and claims that Jesus lived a sinless life, Muslims do not believe that He was God's Son. As a matter of fact, to accept and believe Jesus to be divine is considered blasphemy. The Qur'an vehemently denies that Jesus is the Son of God. Islam proclaims that Jesus was merely a prophet and nothing more.

Doctrine Number 5: Resurrection and Judgment

Both Judaism and Christianity teach that an individual's life ends with physical death, but Muslims do not believe this is so. Authors Bickel and Jantz explain, "Muslims believe that life includes a spiritual dimension that continues after death" (Bickel & Jantz, 2002). The Qur'an teaches that all human deeds are recorded by two angels. When the time comes for an individual to be judged, these angels will assess these recordings on each individual.

Allah then weighs the deeds of each individual on a scale of absolute justice. In this way, each individual's eternal destiny is determined by whether the good deeds outweigh the bad ones, or vice versa. If the good deeds outweigh the bad ones, then this individual will spend eternity in heaven. But if the bad deeds outweigh the good ones, then this individual will spend eternity in hell, a place of unimaginable suffering.

Muslims also believe in resurrection, as do Christians. The Qur'an teaches that believers will see their god, Allah, on the day of resurrection. According to the Qur'an, "Upon that day some faces shall be radiant, gazing upon their Lord" (Sura-75:22–23). It is believed that on judgment day every man and woman from Adam to the last person will be resurrected.

The Sects or Divisions

Although Islam is associated with a variety of sects, the two primary ones are the Sunnis (Orthodox) and the Shi'ites. Some sources estimate that as many as 80 percent of Muslims belong to the Sunnis sect and 15 percent of Muslims belong to the Shi'ites sect.

The Sunnis and Shi'ites differ on some fundamental issues. For example, the Sunnis believe that Muhammad did not appoint anyone to be his successor. Thus they believe that any good Muslim can lead. Conversely, Shi'ites believe that Muhammad appointed Ali, his cousin and son-in-law, to be his successor and leader of the Muslim community. Thus Shi'ites consider Ali to be their first Imam.

Humanity or Human Nature

Islam teaches that human beings are in charge of creation and are under the authority of God. It also teaches that angels imparted the souls or spirits of each individual at the time they were in their mother's womb.

The goal of Islam is to create a moral order in the world. Islam teaches there is no such thing as original sin since humans are born as being good. It also teaches that man's physical nature and animal desires make him vulnerable to wrong doing, and that man's duty is to obey and serve Allah.

Sin

Muslims believe that man by his nature is lost, but he has the ability to choose the right way. They also believe that man can follow his own mistaken ways, worship false gods, and neglect Allah's laws. But in so doing he chooses to suffer the consequences of eternal punishment in hell. Furthermore, they believe that man can choose to repent and submit to Allah, and in doing so he attains Allah's forgiveness.

Author Ron Rhodes notes that "this forgiveness does not require any kind of atonement" (Suras-17:15 & 35:18). Islam is in agreement with Christianity as it relates to the belief that all have sinned. But Islam does not agree with Christianity as it relates to the belief of original sin.

Salvation

According to Islam, an individual's salvation depends on having a belief in Allah and being able to keep the laws of Islam. Thus Islam teaches that an individual's salvation is mainly based on his works, that is, human effort such as carrying out the five pillars. But the Qur'an makes one exception to this teaching, "For those who die as martyrs in war will receive eternal paradise" (Sura-3:157). As mentioned before, an individual's destiny as to whether he will spend eternity in paradise (heaven) or hell is determined by whether good deeds outweigh bad deeds.

Islam further teaches that salvation is the responsibility of each individual and that no one will know his eternal destiny until judgment day. Although human effort plays an essential role in an individual's salvation since salvation is based on works, it is also dependent on the mercy of Allah. For example, Allah can tip the scale of justice in favor of the good side and give the believer hope of entering paradise.

Afterlife

Islam teaches that Allah will someday resurrect all who have died. Every individual will have his life judged by the scale of justice. Thus, depending on how the scale is tipped, an individual will either enter heaven (a place of unimaginable delight) or hell (a place of unimaginable suffering). An individual can choose an eternal destiny in heaven by choosing to live right, ensuring that the good deeds outweigh the bad deeds in the final count.

God in the Qur'an and the Bible

Although the god of the Qur'an and the God of the Bible are not one and the same, as some incorrectly assume, there are some similarities between them. Author Dean Halverson describes these similarities as follows:

1. Both are one.
2. Both are transcendent creators of the universe.
3. Both are sovereign.
4. Both are omnipotent.
5. Both have spoken to humanity through messengers or prophets via angels and also through the written word.
6. Both know in intimate detail the thoughts and deeds of men.
7. Both will judge the wicked.

But the differences between these two religions outnumber these similarities.

CHAPTER 28

CHRISTIANITY COMPARED WITH ISLAM

ISLAM TEACHES THAT there is only one god (Allah), and no partner or son should be associated with him. The Qur'an states that Allah is the creator of the universe (Sura-3:191), and he is sovereign over all (Sura-6:61). Although there are a total of ninety-nine names for Allah, not one of these names is associated with love or loving.

Muslims believe that Allah is so completely unified in terms of self that he cannot be associated with creation. They also believe that Allah's transcendent nature is so extensive that he presents himself as being impersonal. The concept of having both good and evil characteristics stems from Allah, which makes him very unpredictable. Thus it is difficult to discern any true standard of righteousness since it is left up to Allah to choose what he considers to be right and his decision may change since it is not strictly based on a set of principles.

Christianity's Biblical Response

Christianity teaches that there is only one God. But the Christian faith teaches that God is manifested in three persons: the Father, Son, and Holy Spirit. Although the God of Christianity has many names, the names of Jehovah and Yahweh are two names that are very popular. The Bible specifies that God is love (1 John 4:8).

The God of the Bible is considered to be righteous. Furthermore, He maintains a certain standard that does not change, so what He considers to be right is fairly easy to discern and understand. According to Islam, it is considered blasphemous to call Allah Father. Christians call God our Father, which has a positive connotation since this word symbolizes love, compassion, tenderness, understanding, and security.

Jesus

Muslims consider Jesus as being one of the major prophets. Muslims respect and revere Jesus and they agree about His virgin birth. But Muslims do not believe that Jesus was divine or God; rather, they believe that He was merely a messenger of Allah. Furthermore, they believe that it is blasphemy to call Jesus the Son of God. They are convinced that individuals who believe Jesus to be God or the Son of God are infidels or unbelievers.

Islam teaches that although Jesus was a sinless prophet, He was not as great a prophet as Muhammad. Muslims reject the belief that Jesus was crucified. Conversely, they believe that Jesus went directly to heaven and that Judas was crucified instead. Islam teaches that Jesus was created (Sura-3:59), He was human (Sura-3:59), and He was not crucified (Sura-4:157).

Christianity's Biblical Response

The Bible specifies that Jesus is the second person of the Trinity. It also relates that Jesus is the Word that became flesh (John 1:1, 14) and that Jesus is both God and man (Col. 2:9). Jesus claimed to be equal with the Father when He stated, "I and my Father are one" (John 10:30). According to the Bible, Jesus is eternal (Mic. 5:2), is both human and divine (John 1:1, 14), He died on the cross for the sins of mankind (John 1:29; 19:17–18), and He can save human beings (Acts 4:12).

It is unclear how Muslims can deny the teachings of Jesus and yet believe the Bible to be true and Jesus to be a prophet. "To believe that Jesus was just a great man and a prophet is to belittle Him and to deny His own statements. To believe some other man was as great (or greater) as Jesus is to blaspheme Him. If Jesus spoke the Truth, then He was more than a prophet" (Pratte, 2000). Thus Muslims must either believe the divinity or deity of Jesus to be true or they must choose not to believe in Jesus or the Bible as truth.

Holy Spirit

According to Islam, the Holy Spirit is the archangel Gabriel. They also believe Gabriel delivered the words of the Qur'an to Muhammad. Furthermore, they do not believe in the concept of the Holy Spirit as described in the Bible.

Christianity's Biblical Response

According to Christianity, the Holy Spirit is the third person in the Trinity. The Bible specifies that He bears witness to Jesus (John 14:26; 15:26). Christians believe that the Holy Spirit dwells inside each believer. Just before Jesus left the earth after being crucified and resurrected, He promised to send the Holy Spirit as a comforter who would guide Christians into all truth.

Trinity

Islam does not recognize the concept of Trinity. They also believe in the oneness of God and in Allah as the only god. Thus God cannot be either two-in-one or three-in-one. The idea of Trinity is completely rejected and a belief in this concept is considered to be blasphemous.

Christianity's Biblical Response

Christianity teaches that the Trinity does not refer to three gods but rather one God in three persons or manifestations. Both the Old and New Testaments of the Bible support the doctrine of Trinity (Matthew 28:19). Thus an attack against the Trinity is an attack against the deity of Jesus Christ.

Holy Bible

Muslims believe that the Bible has been distorted over time and has been superseded by the Qur'an. Although they perceive the Bible to be the respected word of the prophets, they believe that since it has been distorted, "It is only correct in so far as it agrees with the Qur'an" (Slick, 2008).

The teachings of Muhammad on the Bible are often in contradiction with biblical teachings. Here are some examples of these contradictions:

1. The Qur'an says that one of Noah's sons drowned in the flood (Sura-11:42), (See: Sura-21:76), but the Bible says that all of his sons were spared (Gen. 7:1–7; 1 Peter 3:20).
2. The Qur'an says that Lot's wife stayed behind and perished among the people of Sodom (Sura-26:171), whereas the Bible says that she fled but looked back and was turned into a pillar of salt (Gen. 19:15, 26).
3. The Qur'an teaches that there will be marriage in heaven (Sura-44:54), but Jesus said that there are no marriages in heaven (Matt. 22:30).
4. The Qur'an says that John the Baptist's father was speechless for three days as a sign from the angel (Sura-3:41), but the Bible says that he was speechless from before the time his wife conceived until the baby was born (Luke 1:13, 20, 24, 57–64).

Christianity's Biblical Response

The Bible is believed by Christians to be authentic and divinely inspired. It is the inspired and inerrant Word of God (2 Tim. 3:16). The Bible is the final authority in "all matters of faith and truth" (Halverson, 2003).

The unity found in the Bible is proof that it is God-inspired. For example, despite the fact that forty different men contributed text to the Bible, no one has ever been able to find any contradictions. In addition, there don't appear to be any conflicts between the Old and New Testaments in the areas of its history or geography. Furthermore, the text appears to flow smoothly and continuously.

Muhammad

Islam teaches that Muhammad was the greatest and last prophet that Allah commissioned. Muhammad claimed that he received divine revelations when he was forty years old. Although he was skeptical about the origin or authority of these revelations, his wife convinced him that they came from Allah and were valid. Since Muhammad could neither read nor write he had to dictate these revelations to others who transcribed them. These revelations were then collected and included in the Qur'an.

Christianity's Biblical Response

According to some Christian authors, the authority and authenticity of these revelations in the Qur'an are highly questionable. One such author states, "Non-Muslims believe he developed such a deep religious fervor, out of concern for the needs of the people, that he began having dreams about religion and attributed them to God" (Pratte, 2000). This author further adds that Muhammad's teaching is contradictory against itself, as well as in terms of what the Bible says. Some examples that support this author's conclusion in terms of these apparent contradictions are described below:

1. Although Muhammad said that violence should not be practiced in the name of religion (Sura-2:256), he commanded his disciples to use violence against those who reject Islam (Sura-9:3, 5, 29).
2. First Muhammad taught his followers to pray while they were facing Mecca; then later he taught them to pray while

they were facing Jerusalem (Encyclopedia Britannica, XV-647).

3. Indeed, Muhammad admitted to having changed his teachings at times. Muslim commentators have also identified some five to fifty examples of such apparent discrepancies (Encyclopedia Britannica, XIII-483).

4. Muhammad forbade the use of images at first. Then, while under the threat of starvation, he excused it. Then later he again condemned it.

Despite the fact that the Bible was written by forty different men from different walks of life over many years, it does not contradict itself. Author David E. Pratte further acknowledges that there are no conflicts in history or geography between the Old Testament and the New Testaments. Gospel writers often use Old Testament prophecy and teaching to confirm that the New Testament fulfilled the Old (Pratte, 2000).

Humanity

According to Islam, human beings are good by nature. The Qur'an teaches that man is not made in the image of God (Sura-42:11). It further teaches that man is made out of the dust of the earth (Sura-23:12) and that Allah breathed life into man (Sura-32:9; 15:29). Moreover, it teaches that men and women are born free of sin, that is, there is no such thing as inherited sin or original sin. Thus, Islam does not teach that man has a need for atonement.

Christianity's Biblical Response

The Bible declares that man was created in the image of God (Gen. 1:26). Thus, Christians should not assume that God has a physical body; rather, that man is made in God's image, especially in term of such things as love, faith, and the ability to reason. The Bible also declares that, "all have sinned and come short of the glory of God" (Rom. 3:23). The Bible teaches that human beings are indeed sinners because of original sin due to Adam's fall.

204

Sin

Islam teaches that sin takes place when people reject right guidance or the teachings of the Qur'an. It also teaches that sin can be forgiven through repentance but that no atonement is necessary. Furthermore, Muslims do not believe in the concept of original sin. They also teach that individuals are sinless until they rebel against Allah. In addition, they teach that man by nature does not possess a sinful nature.

Christianity's Biblical Response

The Bible declares that sin can lead to spiritual death (Rom. 6:23). Furthermore, it declares that sin is considered to be moral rebellion against a holy God. It also supports the belief in man's need for atonement. Accordingly, the nature of human beings' sinfulness originated with Adam and then was passed down from parent to the child. The Bible states, "Were by nature children of wrath" (Eph. 2:3). Moreover, the Bible declares, "all have sinned" except Jesus, and that Jesus is the only one who was sinless.

Salvation

The Qur'an teaches that salvation can be attained by sincerity and good works; it is earned through a life of good deeds. The Qur'an further teaches that Allah's grace can forgive sin and there is no need of any mediator. One author states, "The Muslims must believe Allah exists, believe in the fundamental doctrines of Islam, believe that Muhammad is his prophet, and follow the commands of Allah given in the Qur'an" (Slick, 2008). The Qur'an also teaches that the concept of salvation is based on our good deeds outweighing the bad ones; it is based on human effort, or works.

Authors Ankerberg and Burroughs state that according to Islam, "Salvation is completely based on human effort, especially the practice of the five pillars and the articles of faith." (Ankerberg, J. & Burroughs, D., 2008). A consideration of the following quotes from the Qur'an further supports the belief that Muslims strongly believe that Jesus cannot play any part in an individual's salvation: "For those things that are good, remove those that are evil" (Sura-11:114); and "one exception is that those who die as martyrs in war will receive eternal paradise" (Sura-3:157).

Christianity's Biblical Response

The Bible teaches that an individual's salvation cannot be earned by human effort. It is given to human beings as a free gift by way of God's grace which human beings receive through faith (Eph. 2:8–9). The Bible also teaches that Jesus acts as the mediator between God and man (1 Tim. 2:5). In addition, the Bible teaches that "our righteousnesses are like filthy rags" (Isa. 64:6, NKJV). Thus human beings are hopelessly lost without a Savior. The Bible also declares that in order to redeem mankind, "God gave his only begotten Son, that whosoever believeth in him should not perish, but have everlasting life" (John 3:16).

Afterlife

Islam teaches that the status of an individual's life at the time of his death is based on whether his good deeds outweigh his bad deeds, or vice versa. Accordingly, those with more good deeds than bad ones will go to heaven (paradise) and those with more bad deeds than good ones will go to hell (pain and suffering). The Qur'an describes the afterlife as a life in paradise (Sura-29:58; Sura-75:12) for faithful Muslims and a place of hell (Sura-29:23) for infidels or unbelievers of Islam.

Christianity's Biblical Response

The Bible teaches that individuals who die enter either heaven or hell based on whether or not they are saved at the time of their death. The Bible declares that when Christians (or believers) die they will be with the Lord in heaven (Phil. 1:21–24) and that when they are in heaven they will be in their glorified or resurrected bodies (1 Cor. 15:50–58). Conversely, the Bible explains that when non-Christians (or unbelievers) die, they will be cast into hell (lake of fire) forever (Matthew-25:41–46).

The Conclusion

Although the religion of Islam and Christianity may agree on some things, the differences between these two beliefs are irreconcilable. Christians and Muslims are not worshipping the same God. Furthermore, these are "two religious systems with radically different beliefs and two different Gods" (Ankerberg and Burroughs, 2008). To suggest that these two belief systems believe in following the same God is simply not accurate. Moreover, the Bible does not support this belief.

There are many apparent contradictions in the Qur'an in terms of what the Bible says as well as in terms of what Muslims believe. For example, Muslims claim that Muhammad also lived a sinless life; he never sinned. Author David E. Pratte carefully researched and compared the life of Muhammad to that of Jesus and noted the following contradictions in his article *Islam Versus Christianity* (The Gospel Way.com).

Broken Treaties:

1. While ruling in Medina, Muhammad made a treaty not to attack Mecca for ten years. He attacked them the following year (Christian Response to Islam by William Miller, 33).

Violence and Assassination

2. Muhammad used violence, including assassination, to defeat and convert men to Islam (World Religions by Norman Anderson, 98; Encyclopedia Britannica, XV-648).

Polygamy

3. Muhammad had twelve wives and two concubines at the time of his death (Christian Response to Islam by William Miller, 32).

Revelations for Personal Benefit and Convenience

4. It is important to note that Muslims can marry the divorced wives of adopted sons (Sura-33:37), and yet it is forbidden to adopt sons (Sura-33:4-5).
5. Muhammad revealed that men could have plural wives, but not more than four at a time (Sura-4:3). However, a special revelation allowed him to have more than four wives. He had twelve wives when he died (Sura-33:50–51).
6. Arabs once starved him because they opposed his teachings against idolatry. He then received a revelation condoning idolatry. As soon as they released him, he reversed this revelation so that the practice of idolatry was again considered to be wrong (Encyclopedia Britannica, XV-647).

Muhammad Himself Never Claimed to Be Sinless

7. Muhammad admitted that he and other prophets had committed sin. But he never claimed that Jesus sinned (Christian Response to Islam by William Miller, 26; World Religions by Norman Anderson, 99).

Both Christians and Muslims agree that Jesus was sinless. The Qur'an does not claim that Jesus sinned (Sura-3:46; 6:85; 19:19). Evidence shows that the reader has good reason to doubt that Muhammad was without sin. Based on character and the evidence presented, was Muhammad or Jesus the greater prophet? I believe that the truth speaks for itself.

Muhammad Did Not Perform Any Miracles

Contrary to the belief by some Muslims, Muhammad did not perform any miracles during his life. Furthermore, there have been no eyewitnesses to confirm that he ever performed any miracles. The Qur'an does not mention that he ever performed any supernatural acts.

When asked why he did not perform any miracles, Muhammad stated that the creation of the Qur'an was his miracle (Sura-29:48–50). Surprisingly though, the Qur'an does record that Muhammad refused to do miracles (Sura-3:181–184; Sura-4:153; Sura-6:8, 9).

One author describes that "most of the individuals who collected miracle stories about Muhammad lived between 100 and 200 years after Muhammad's time, meaning, they were not eyewitness to Muhammad's life" (Rhodes, 2002). Another author states, "One night Muhammad was allegedly carried to Jerusalem and from there ascended into heaven to see wonderful visions. However, no one saw it happen. His wife says he never left the bed" (Christian Response to Islam by William Miller, 24), (Pratte, 2000).

Qur'an's Beauty and Eloquence Does Not Prove It Is Divine

Due to its beauty and eloquence, Muslims believe that Allah authored the Qur'an. But beauty and eloquence do not provide a reasonable test to determine divine inspiration. If this were true, then many other authors with works of beauty and eloquence such as Bach, Beethoven, Mozart, Oscar Wilde, and Shakespeare could claim them to be divinely inspired as well.

One reasonable objection to refute the claim of the Qur'an's being beautiful and eloquent is that it possesses many grammatical errors. Christian Apologist, Ravi Zacharias stated:

> Let us consider just one troublesome aspect, the grammatical flaws that have been demonstrated. Ali Dashti, an Iranian author and a committed Muslim, commented that the errors in the Qur'an were so many that the grammatical rules had to be altered in order to fit the claim that the Qur'an was flawless. He gives numerous examples of these in his book, *Twenty-three years: The Life of the Prophet Muhammad.* (The only precaution he took before publishing this book was to direct that it be published posthumously).
>
> —Zacharias, 2000

Author Ali Dashti wisely chose to make arrangements for his book to be published after his death since if he had chosen to publish his book while he was still alive, he most assuredly would have been marked for death (like many others). In this book, he wrote:

> The Qur'an contains sentences which are incomplete and not fully intelligible without the aid of commentaries; foreign words, unfamiliar Arabic words, and words used with other than the normal meaning; adjectives and verbs inflected without observance of the concord of gender and number; illogical and ungrammatically applied pronouns which sometimes have no referent; and remote from the subjects. These and other such aberrations in the language have given scope to critics who deny the Qur'an's eloquence. To sum up, more than 100 Qur'anic aberrations from the normal rules and structure of Arabic have been noted.
> —Dashti, 1985

Is the Qur'an Really God's Word?

There are too many contradictions between the Qur'an and the Bible to make the claim that both came from God. Muslims have tried to convince individuals that the Qur'an has been accurately preserved, and they strongly insist that the Bible has been distorted. Thus, Muslins claim that where conflicts are found to exist between the Bible and the Qur'an, only what is stated in the Qur'an is accurate.

One author described some of the most notable contradictions between the Qur'an and the Bible in his book *Reasoning from the Scriptures with Muslims* (Ron Rhodes, 2002). The following quotes appeared in his book:

1. Genesis 8:4 says Noah's ark rested on the mountains of Ararat, while the Qur'an says Noah's ark rested on Mount Judi (Sura-11:44).
2. Genesis 11:27 says Terah was Abraham's father, whereas the Qur'an says Azar was his father (Sura-6:74).

3. Exodus 2:5 says the daughter of Pharaoh found the baby Moses in an ark and adopted him as her son, while the Qur'an says Pharaoh's wife adopted Moses (Sura-28:8-9).
4. Matthew 27:35 says Jesus was crucified, while the Qur'an says He was not crucified nor even killed (Sura-4:157).
5. Luke 1:20 indicates Zechariah's punishment for doubt was that he would not be able to speak until his son was born, while the Qur'an says he would not be able to speak for three nights (Sura-3:41; 19:10).
6. Luke 2:6–7 says Mary gave birth to Jesus in a stable, whereas the Qur'an says she gave birth under a palm tree (Sura-19:23).
7. Hebrews 1:1–3 indicates that Jesus is the brightness of God's glory and the express image of His person, while the Qur'an says Jesus was no more than a messenger (Sura-5:75).
8. John 3:16 says God loves all people, while the Qur'an says Allah loves only those who follow him (Sura-3:32, 57).
9. Romans 5:8 indicates that God loves even sinners, while the Qur'an indicates that Allah does not love transgressors (Sura-2:190).
10. Ephesians 5:25-28 says husbands are to love their wives as Christ loved the church, whereas the Qur'an says husbands can beat their wives if there is reason for it (Sura-4:34).

Other Notable Contradictions

1. One day in the life of Allah equals 1,000 years (Sura-22:47; 32:5) or is it 50,000 years (Sura-70:4)?
2. Did Allah create the earth in six days (Sura-7:54; 10:3; 11:7; 25:59) or in eight days (Sura-41:9–12)?
3. Words of Allah cannot be changed (Sura-6:34; 6:115) or does Allah substitute one revelation for another (Sura-2:106; 16:101)?

4. How many angels were talking to Mary (Jesus' mother)? Is it just one angel (Sura-19:17-21) or were there several angels (Sura-3:42, 45)?

5. How many gardens are there in paradise? Only one garden (Sura-39:73; 57:21; 79:41) or are there several gardens (Sura-18:31; 22:23; 35:33; 78:32)?

6. Does the angel Gabriel bring forth the revelation from Allah to Muhammad (Sura-2:97) or is it the Holy Spirit who brings forth the revelation (Sura-16:102)?

7. How many groups will be there at the last judgment? Two groups (Sura-90:18-19; Sura-99:6-8), or will there be three groups (Sura-56:7)?

8. Where does good and evil in our life come from? Is it from Satan (Sura-4:117-120) or is it from Allah (Sura-4:78) or is it from ourselves (Sura-4:79)?

9. Who takes people's souls at death? The angel of death (Sura-32:11) or the angels (plural)—(Sura-47:27), or is it Allah that takes the souls at death (Sura-39:42)?

10. Holy Qur'an is in clear Arabic speech (Sura-16:103) and men of understanding do grasp it (Sura-3:7). Then how come none knows its interpretation save only Allah (Sura-3:7)?

11. How many wings do angels have? Do angels have two, three, or four pairs of wings (Sura-35:1)? It has been said that angel Gabriel had 600 wings (Source: Mr. Sahih Bukhari, Volume-4, Book-54, Number-455).

12. Does God need man (Sura-51:56)? Or does man need God (Sura-35:15)?

13. Which part of the human enters the paradise? Is it the body (Sura-17:98-99; 20:55; 75:3-4) or is it the soul (Sura-31:28; 89:27-30) or is it both?

14. How many days did Allah need to destroy the people of Aad? Was it just one day (Sura-54:19) or was it several days (Sura-41:16; 69:6-7)?

15. Which was created first, the heavens or the earth? Was the earth created first (Sura-2:29) or were the heavens created first (Sura-79:27-30)?

16. Does Allah forgive Shrik? No (Sura-4:48; 4:116), or Yes (Sura-4:153; 25:68–71)?

17. In Sura-18:89-98, we read that Alexander the Great was a devout Muslim and lived to a ripe old age. However, historical records show that Alexander the Great died at a young age of 32 years.

18. Who should be blamed for belief and for unbelief (Sura-6:12) and (Sura-10:100)?

19. What is the attitude towards unbelieving parents (Sura-9:23) and (Sura-31:15)?

20. God's advice to Muhammad on propagating Islam: (Sura-2:256; 3:20; 8:38-39).

21. Who can be blamed for the wrongs done (Sura-4:79; 30:9) or (Sura-2:142; 16:93; 35:8; 74:31)?

22. The Qur'an was written in pure Arabic (Sura-12:2; 13:37; 16:103; 41:41, 44). It has been said that there are numerous foreign words in it such as: Aramaic, Assyrian, Egyptian, Ethiopian, Greek, Hebrew, Persian, and Syriac.

23. Should unbelievers be persecuted or forgiven (Sura-9:29; 98:6) or (Sura-16:128; 45:14)?

24. Could Allah have a son? In Sura-39:4, we read that Allah could, if he wished it and yet Sura-6:101 denies it.

25. Who misleads people: Allah (Sura-16:93) or Satan (Sura-4:119-20)?

26. If the inheritance laws provides an equal share for women and men (Sura-4:7), then why is it doubled for men (Sura-4:11; 4:176)?

27. Is the punishment for an adulteress life imprisonment (Sura-4:15) or is it 100 strokes by flogging (Sura-24:2)?

28. Why is it that homosexuals are let off if they repent (Sura-4:16), though the same allowance is not given for heterosexuals (Sura-24:2)?

29. Wine is considered to be Satan's handiwork (Sura-5:90); yet there are rivers of wine in paradise (Sura-47:15; 83:25). How does Satan's handiwork get into paradise?

30. If the Bible is considered authoritative (Sura-4:136; 5:68; 21:7; 29:46), then why is so much of it (the Bible) contradicted by the Qur'an (Sura-5:73–75; 5:116)?

Muslims clearly make many favorable claims in terms of Islam by presenting it to be true and genuine. Although making a claim is not that difficult and just about anyone can do so, the challenge is in proving it. All of the teachings of Jesus are in agreement with themselves, but there are many contradictions concerning the teachings of Muhammad.

A Final Note

Many facts on Islam and the Qur'an have been presented. Concerning these facts, all an individual needs to do is to let the truth speak for itself. But witnessing to Muslims about Christ requires much more than just sharing a personal testimony or convincing theological and spiritual arguments. Rather, it necessitates spiritual warfare. Furthermore, the struggle of Christian believers is not against flesh and blood, or Muslims, Buddhists, Hindus, or any other people from other religious (or non-religious) faiths. Rather, the Christian's struggle is against "principalities and powers that hold these people in bondage" (Safa, 1996). The apostle Paul wrote, "For we wrestle not against flesh and blood, but against principalities, against powers, against the rulers of the darkness of this world, against spiritual wickedness in high places" (Eph. 6:12).

How then do Christians take on such an enormous task? Although it is not easy, it is possible only with God's help and mercy. Christian believers can be successful in fulfilling their obligations toward winning others to Christ by praying, fasting, and interceding on behalf of all non-believers. Thus Christians should set aside a lot of quality time to pray and intercede on behalf of people not yet saved (possibly family members), as well as for those who belong to the Christian faith.

The Bible states that those who are seeking to know God need to "seek the LORD while He may be found" (Isa. 55:6, NKJV). It further states, "Behold, now is the day of salvation" (2 Cor. 6:2). Thus it is highly recommended that those individuals who are not yet saved seriously consider studying and finding out about Jesus and His plan for salvation since no one knows just how long he will live, and his decision to accept or reject Christ as Lord and Savior is a decision that will affect where he will spend eternity (heaven or hell).

Unfortunately, there will be many who choose to rebel and reject Christ and His free gift of salvation. But when individuals stand alone before God on judgment day, they will acknowledge Jesus as Lord, as stated in the Bible: "Wherefore God also hath highly exalted him, and given him a name which is above every name: that at the name of Jesus every knee should bow, of things in heaven, and things in earth, and things under the earth; and that every tongue should confess that Jesus Christ is Lord, to the glory of God the Father" (Phil. 2:9–11).

SECTION SIX

CHRISTIAN APOLOGETICS

CHAPTER 29

DEFENDING THE FAITH

HOW DOES AN individual define apologetics and why should anyone spend time studying it? The term apologetics is derived from the Greek word "apologia," which means *defense*. According to Ravi Zacharias, noted Christian author and apologist, an apologist is not defined as an individual who constantly apologizes. Rather, it is the part of Christian theology that involves the reasoning and intelligent "presentation and defense of the historical Christian faith" (Apologeticsindex.com). This reasoning and intelligent defense is targeted to enlighten both Christians and unbelievers.

Today Christianity is being attacked more than ever before, and individuals must seek to defend it not only based on reasoning but scripturally as well. Those attacking Christianity come from both inside and outside the church. The challenges linked to these attacks involve such aspects as cults, heresies, the occult, and sects. But the majority of challenges that come from outside the church involve such aspects as agnosticism, atheism, humanistic secularism, the new age movement, and skepticism from other religions.

Skeptics seem to have many objections and questions when it comes to the Bible and the Christian faith. Christians need to study the Bible in order to be ready to provide an answer to these objections and questions. The Bible encourages Christian believers to be ready in season and out of season to give answers concerning God's word, as it states, "be ready always to give an answer to every man that asketh you a reason of the hope that is in you with meekness and fear" (1 Peter 3:15).

The primary way that a believer can prepare himself to be able to answer any question or objection that another individual might have is by studying what other religions teach and believe. This type of study falls under the area of apologetics.

What then is the goal of apologetics? According to author Steven B. Cowan, "The goal of apologetics is to persuasively answer honest objections that keep people from faith in Jesus Christ" (Cowan, 2008). So many different religions are in existence today, and although these religions may have some teachings in common, their differences far outweigh their similarities. Furthermore, many of the teachings of other religions contradict one another. And each of these different religions offers a different means by which individuals can come to God.

With so many contradictions among other religions and the resulting confusion, how should a believer best approach these seeming discrepancies and what should a believer say about other religions? If the claim that Jesus is God in the flesh is true, then whatever Jesus says must be considered to be authoritative. Jesus clearly stated, "I am the way, the truth, and the life. No one comes to the Father except through Me" (John 14:6, NKJV). If this statement holds true, then other claims to this effect from any other individual or the god of any other religion must be false.

Why should nonbelievers have faith in Christ over all other religions? This question haunted me for quite some time during my search for the truth as it related to God. Before I came to Christ, I was a diehard skeptic. I underscored my skepticism by making a long list of questions and objections. And I excelled at debating all who would dare to challenge my belief in Hinduism. But at the same time, deep down within myself I was genuinely hoping that, through all of these debates, I would ultimately come to know the truth as it related to God.

Due to being born into a Hindu Brahmin family, I was very preoccupied with the Hindu way of life, Thus I was steadfastly determined to remain loyal to my heritage and maintain my resolve to not let anything get in the way of keeping to the religion of my Hindu background. But the emptiness and spiritual loneliness that I was experiencing far outweighed in importance the questions and objections that I had in terms of Christianity. Thus I decided to keep an open mind and be objective rather than to just outright reject what others told me about their faith.

Some individuals first want to make sure that their questions get answered before they consider accepting Christ as their Lord and Savior. Furthermore, non-Christians often look to Christians to see if they have adequate knowledge to answer their questions. Christians should do their best to educate themselves in terms of what other individuals believe or don't believe, as well as in terms of what Christians believe. Some common objections and questions that skeptics often present to Christians are discussed below.

Common Questions Skeptics Ask or Objections People Have

Nonbelievers commonly object to or question the areas of Christianity that deal with God, Jesus, the Bible, and Man (humanity), Christianity, Christians, sin, and religion.

Question Number 1: If God exists, why is there so much evil in the world?

Christian Response

The basis for this frequently asked question usually stems from the fact that the Bible portrays God to be holy, perfect, and righteous. But the answer to this question is quite straightforward: When God created mankind and the universe, everything was perfect since there was no sin (or evil). Sin entered the world only when Adam and Eve chose to disobey God.

Until Jesus returns and the world is renewed, evil will always be prevalent. God gives individuals a free will in terms of choosing to obey Him. Human beings have the option to make wrong choices, whether their choices are due to rebelliousness, selfishness, or ignorance. Sometimes God allows evil to impact an individual in order for that person to learn a life lesson. But the solution for sin (evil) was provided when Jesus defeated death on the Cross.

Question Number 2: If God exists, why do we have so much suffering in the world?

Christianity's Biblical Response

Pain and suffering are related in that they both can lead to stress. But stress can be both good and bad. Author Frank Harber states, "Pain is an essential mechanism for survival. Without pain the body is stripped of vital protection. Pain is an important signal to warn of even greater danger" (Christianity Today, 2000). Similarly, suffering may also bring about good because it can often indicate that an individual needs to make changes. The noted Christian apologist C.S. Lewis stated, "God whispers to us in our pleasure, speaks to us in our conscience, but shouts to us in our pain; it is His megaphone to rouse a deaf world."

Individuals can draw comfort in knowing that regardless of any pain and suffering they may have to endure God will cause "all things [to] work together for good to those who love God" (Rom. 8:28, NKJV). I believe the reason suffering comes to so many people is because they choose to take God's grace and mercy for granted. And yet these same individuals are surprised or even disturbed when suffering comes their way. For instance, we read in Galatians-6:7, "Do not be deceived, God is not mocked; for whatever a man sows, that he will also reap." This Scripture is a good reminder to all of us that sin does and will have its own consequence. God is a forgiving God. But He is also a just and holy God, meaning, He will deal with sins in a just fashion.

Question Number 3: If God exists and He is a loving God, why would He send human beings to hell?

Christian Response

Although evil, pain, and suffering appear to be long lasting, these effects are all temporary and will cease one day for all those who accept Jesus as their Lord and Savior and His free gift of salvation. God does not send anyone to hell. Rather, individuals choose to go to hell on their own accord…by not asking Jesus to forgive their sin, not believing that Jesus died on the cross to pay the penalty for their sin, and not choosing to receive His gift of eternal life. Since God is a just God, He must judge sin.

Question Number 4: Why is Jesus the only way to gain access to God?

Christianity's Biblical Response

Jesus stated, "I am the way, the truth, and the life. No one comes to the Father except through Me" (John 14:6. NKJV). His claim of being God is based both on what He did and on who He claimed to be. An individual only has to study what Jesus did to be able to determine who He was. For example, He forgave sins (Luke 5:20), He rose from the dead (John 20:11–18), and He raised others from the dead (John11:43 44). He also walked on water (John-6:19), healed the sick (the leper), gave sight to the blind, fed several thousand with only a few fish and loaves of bread, and turned water into wine. No one on earth has ever done those things before, and this is what makes Jesus so special.

Question Number 5: Why did Jesus have to die in order for me to go to heaven?

Christianity's Biblical Response

The Bible states that "all have sinned, and come short of the glory of God" (Rom. 3:23) and that "the wages of sin is death" (Rom. 6:23).

Although Jesus never sinned (1 Peter 2:22), He paid the penalty for the sins of mankind by sacrificing Himself on the cross (1 Peter 2:24) and, thus, He chose to die in place of all human beings. The Bible clearly states that God hates sin (Hab. 1:13) and that sin separates us from God (Isa. 59:2). God offered Jesus to die in place of all human beings for their sins, and there was no other way to pay for the wages of sin.

Question Number 6: Isn't the Bible filled with errors?

Christianity's Biblical Response

The Bible is the Word of God, and God by His nature does not lie (John 17:17). The Bible is truth and can be taken at face value. Author Harber states, "What most people claim as errors in the Bible aren't errors but difficulties. People think they have stumbled upon apparent inconsistencies when they haven't taken the time to find out all the facts or make an in-depth study of the passage" (Christianity Today, 2000). No errors can be found in the Bible; it is often best described as "the word of truth" (2 Tim. 3:16).

Question Number 7: Does the Bible contradict itself?

Christian Response

Two different accounts of events do not mean that they are contradictory. There are many examples in the Bible that prove this such as the account of Jesus' birth as described in Matthew and Luke. Christian author, Rusty Wright (Probe.org) states, "The gospels never claim to be exhaustive records. Biographers must be selective. The accounts seem complementary, not contradictory." The Bible has been tested by time and it should be trusted based on its trustworthiness.

Question Number 8: Isn't Christianity a psychological crutch?

Christianity's Biblical Response

Nonbelievers often think that Christianity is for weaklings. They think that Christians are usually emotionally unstable and require some type of support in order to satisfy their emotional instability. Christians are strong not in their own strength but as they fully gain their strength from Jesus. The Bible states that when we are weak, we are made strong in Him (see 2 Cor. 12: 10).

Every human being has a need for some type of assistance. But to whom do we turn for help when we need assistance? Mankind is capable of doing only so much, and man does not always have the answers. Author Harber states that "Christianity provides what atheism or other religions never can: spiritual fulfillment, peace, and forgiveness" (Christianity Today, 2000). Moreover, Christianity promises to satisfy the needs of human beings such as love, forgiveness, grace, compassion, identity (to be a child of God), and worth.

Question Number 9: Isn't Christianity boring?

Christian Response

Born-again believers do not find Christianity boring. Rather, it is usually individuals who have never experienced having been born again who think that it must be boring to follow Jesus. Based on my personal experience, I have found that being a Christian can be a lot of fun and I try to enjoy every minute of life to the best of my ability. Some individuals think that time goes fast when one is having fun. Christians do not just read the Bible and pray all day long, as some wrongly think. We enjoy all aspects of like such as reading, sports, education, and developing relationships. Yet they also face the same problems as individuals who are not born again believers. The difference is that they have God in their lives to help them in life. The life of a Christian is full of adventure and is not boring.

Questions Number 10: Aren't Christians hypocrites?

Christianity's Biblical Response

Hypocrisy exists in every religion and cult and in every part of any culture. Nothing in this world is perfect, except for God.

Unfortunately, some well-known and highly respected Christian leaders have proven themselves to be bad examples of what a Christian is by acting as hypocrites. Individuals should never look to other human beings as being primary examples of what Christianity or a Christian should be.

Jesus expects His disciples to follow Him and no one else, regardless of their name, fame, status, power, and educational or financial credentials. Since human beings have a sin nature, they are prone to failure. They should never be looked up to as being perfect examples to follow. The obvious question to ask is, was Jesus a hypocrite? The answer to this question is unequivocally "No." Furthermore, the Bible presents Jesus as being nothing less than perfect. Jesus Himself challenged others to prove that He'd ever sinned (John 8:46).

Question Number 11: What about the atrocities that have been committed in the name of Christ?

Christianity's Biblical Response

Unfortunately and sadly, millions of people have died in the name of crusades, slavery, and wars. Oftentimes Christians have been blamed and accused of doing such horrendous atrocities associated with these events. But it is not right or fair to blame everyone when only a few who claim to be Christians are guilty of such acts. Jesus taught that by their fruits we shall know them (see Matt. 7:15–20). If the fruit is not consistent with what Jesus taught, that person probably has never surrendered his life to Jesus as Savior and Lord.

For example, many so-called professing Christians both in the past and present who are believers in name only (hypocrites) and are not born again of the Spirit of God (the only true Christians). The Bible clearly states that Jesus Himself will say to these hypocrites that, "I never knew you; depart from Me, you who practice lawlessness" (Matt. 7:23, NKJV).

A lot of atrocities that cost the lives of many have taken place in the name of Christianity and religion. Conversely, there has been a lot of good done in the name of Christ by true followers over the years, including building colleges, charity agencies, hospitals, orphanages, and relief agencies.

Question Number 12: There is no such thing as sin!

Christianity's Biblical Response

Those individuals who think there is no sin are indirectly saying that there is no God. The Bible defines sin as an act of rebellion or disobedience against a holy God. Furthermore, the Bible tells us that sin is doing what is wrong before God (see 1 John 3:4). All that an individual has to do to prove the existence of sin is to evaluate his own life in terms of such aspects as anger, cheating, deception, envy, jealousness, lying, murder, and stealing. And there are many other ways to prove the existence of sin. We only have to look around us at our world.

Question Number 13: I am already good enough and I do not consider myself to be a bad person!

Christianity's Biblical Response

Because God is holy and human beings are made in the image of God, humans are required to be holy. But since human beings are born with a sin nature, they cannot be holy like God. Humans are constantly sinning because of their sin nature. And sin separates human beings from God. How good do humans need to be in order to get to heaven? A single sin can disqualify humans from enjoying a personal relationship with God.

Furthermore, God knows that humans can never be good enough based on their own effort. That is why He sent Jesus (who was sinless) to die on behalf of all mankind and to redeem mankind so that they could choose to repent of their sin, ask Christ to forgive their sin (be the propitiation for their sin), and then receive His free gift of salvation by asking Him to come into their hearts and making Him their Lord and Savior.

The Bible clearly states that no one is good enough to make it to heaven by his own accord: "There is none who does good, no not one" (Rom. 3:12, NKJV). God is not subject to human reasoning. Rather, humans are subject to His reasoning. Thus the goodness of human beings is measured not according to their standards but by God's standards. In fact, by believing that an individual is good enough is another way to say that Jesus died in vain or for no reason. The Bible clearly states, "for if righteousness comes through the law, then Christ died in vain" (Gal. 2:21, NKJV).

Question Number 14: I am an atheist; I don't believe in God!

Christianity's Biblical Response

There are two ways that an individual can be an atheist: "someone who says he believes there is no God, and someone who simply lacks a belief in God. An atheist cannot say that he knows there is no God, because he would have to know all things in order to know if there is or isn't God" (Slick, 2008). The Bible gives many logical reasons for the existence of God. One such example is His creation. Creation is proof that God exists because something cannot come from nothing. We read in the Bible that, "God created the world out of nothing" (Job-38:4–39:5).

Question Number 15: Since all religions are good it does not matter what you believe.

Christian Response

It is true that all religions may share some commonalities, but not all of them can be true. Furthermore, not all religions have in common the same path to the same God. Indeed, all religions do not agree and teach about the same God. This is evident since there are many contradictions in the beliefs of the other religions. Truth is powerful and it does not contradict itself.

For example, Hindus believe in reincarnation, Buddhists do not believe in a personal God, Muslims accept Jesus only as a prophet, and Christianity claims that there is a personal God and that Christians can have a personal relationship with Him through Jesus (John 14:6). Thus these religions (and all others) cannot be different paths to the same God since they contradict one another. Truth does not contradict itself, and there are no contradictions found in the Word of God (the Bible).

Question Number 16: I don't need religion

Christian Response

In his book *Reason to Believe* author R. C. Sproul states that people think religion is a crutch for those who are not strong enough to cope with the pressures of life. They don't feel the need for religion. They say, "My life is going smoothly"; or, "Why can't you stand on your own two feet?" To the believer in Christ, Christianity is not considered a religion. Rather, it is a personal one-on-one relationship with Jesus.

Question Number 17: What happens to those who have never heard of Jesus?

Christianity's Biblical Response

The Bible states, "to him that knoweth to do good, and doeth it not, to him it is sin" (James 4:17). In order for people to sin, they need to know what sin is and how they commit it. If an individual chooses to sin once he knows what it is, then it can be considered as an act of rebellion or sin. The same Scripture may also be applied to those who are mentally challenged at birth, as is often the case with such maladies as Down Syndrome, and also with young children who may not understand the concept of sin and salvation. When these individuals die, I believe that they will be forgiven by grace since it is not their fault that they do not understand the concept of life, sin, salvation, heaven, and hell. I believe that God judges each individual in accordance with the knowledge he or she possesses at death.

CHAPTER 30

WHAT IS GOD LIKE?

MANY INDIVIDUALS QUESTION, "Who made God?" Noted Christian apologists and authors Geisler and Zacharias state, "No one made God. He was not made. He has always existed. Only the things that had a beginning—like the world—need a maker. God had no beginning, so God did not need to be made" (Geisler & Zacharias, 2003). God's many miracles include such things as the creation of heaven, earth, and human beings. The Bible states, "In the beginning God created the heaven and the earth" (Gen. 1:1).

Many individuals also question the nature of God, that is, His attributes or characteristics. Furthermore, they view the God of the Old Testament as a God of hate, wrath, or anger, and think that the God of the New Testament is a God of love, compassion, mercy, and forgiveness.

Two Old Testament events that identify God as being wrathful include the great flood during the time of Noah and the destruction of Sodom and Gomorrah. Conversely, God in the New Testament has been portrayed as the God who shows love, forgiveness, and mercy. But Jesus Himself stated that the Old Testament may be summed up by the two commandments to love God and to love your neighbor (Matt. 22:37–40). Skeptics also question how God can be both just and loving at the same time.

The God of the Old Testament does not desire to judge and bring wrath. The Bible states, "'Do I have any pleasure at all that the wicked should die?' says the Lord God, 'and not that he should turn from his ways and live'" (Ezek. 18:23, NKJV)? The New Testament Scriptures twice confirm this to be the case. "I desire mercy and not sacrifice" (Matt. 9:13; 2:7, NKJV). Yet God is a God who must judge and He must punish sin.

An analogy that I frequently use to help individuals understand the concept of the duality of justice and love is as follows: A certain state trooper had a son who loved to drive fast on the highway and often went well over the speed limit. One day his father stopped him and issued a ticket, which surprised the son because he was expecting some kind of break from his dad. The dad told his son that as a father he was willing to forgive him for the speeding, but as an officer of the law, even though he was his son, he had to issue him a ticket.

Even though God forgives sins upon confession, every sin brings about consequences. In the example of the state trooper, although the dad was both loving and forgiving, he had an obligation to uphold the law by being just. God operates in a similar fashion. None of the characteristics of God are contradictory; rather, they complement each other.

Who Is Jesus?

The Bible repeatedly states that Jesus is God. One such example states that "I and my Father are one" (John 10:30). And there are many other such claims in the Bible. They are either true or false. C. S. Lewis, noted author, scholar, and Christian apologist, stated in his book *Mere Christianity* that Jesus can only be one of three things: a liar, a lunatic, or simply Lord.

Was Jesus a liar? Jesus was lying if He knew that He was not God when He claimed to be God. Furthermore, if He was lying then He was also a hypocrite since He had previously told others to be honest and sincere at any cost. Moreover, it would not be reasonable for Him to live a lie while encouraging others to tell the truth when, in fact, He said, "You shall know the truth, and the truth shall make you free" (John 8:32, NKJV). There is not a single incident where Jesus was caught lying or sinning. To believe Him to be lying about His claim to be God would be counter to the portrayal of His character throughout the Bible.

Conversely, when Jesus was being challenged by religious leaders regarding His claim to be God, His complete innocence in the matter was acknowledged approximately eleven times. If He was a liar, it should have been easy for others to expose Him as such. Obviously, His disciples did not believe His claims to be a lie, otherwise they would most likely have left Him and returned to what they were doing before they met Him. Instead, they continued following Him. The Bible records that even Pontius Pilate, the Roman governor, was not able to find any fault with Jesus. Jesus was not a liar.

If Jesus was not a liar, was He a lunatic who claimed to be deity (God)? The Bible does not record any evidence that Jesus' behavior in dealing with people is considered lunacy. Furthermore, His teachings, which are considered to be ethical and moral, do not indicate that they came from someone suffering from a mental defect. Rather, His teachings were bringing human beings closer to God.

Although other religions may not accept Jesus as God, they do acknowledge that He was a great teacher and humanitarian. Author and Christian apologist Josh McDowell notes that "Jesus was not only sane, but also the counsel He provides gives us the most concise and accurate formula for peace of mind and heart" (McDowell, 2006).

If Jesus was neither a liar nor a lunatic, then He must be the Lord since all credible evidence supports this belief. Those who were closest to Him and knew Him best should have been able to pick up on any sort of misgivings in terms of His sincerity. Yet, they concluded:

- "And Simon Peter answered and said, Thou art the Christ, the Son of the living God. And Jesus answered and said unto him, Blessed art thou, Simon Barjona: for flesh and blood hath not revealed it unto thee, but my Father which is in heaven" (Matt. 16:16–17).

- "And Thomas answered and said unto him, My Lord and my God" (John 20:28).
- "The beginning of the gospel of Jesus Christ, the Son of God" (Mark 1:1).

There have been so many self-proclaimed gods and saviors that have come and gone, but Jesus is still here and He is here to stay. The evidence that has been presented clearly points in favor of Jesus as Lord. Now, because the facts are presented and evidence shown, the next most important question (that has eternal significance) to ask is: "What do I do with this truth?"

Old Testament Prophecies about Jesus Christ Fulfilled in the New Testament

Although the Old Testament (also known as the Hebrew Bible) was written hundreds of years before the birth of Jesus, and the New Testament was written after Jesus' death and resurrection, there are at least 100 prophecies in the Old Testament that address the deity of Jesus. Some were prophesied more than 1,200 years before the birth of Jesus; some were prophesied 800 years before and some were 500 years before His birth.

No other founder of any religion can claim this kind of prophetic fulfillment. Jesus is uniquely different, fascinating, and amazing. Some of the significant Old Testament prophecies about Jesus that have already been fulfilled as shown in the New Testament are presented below:

1. Born of a virgin – Isaiah 7:14 (OT); Matthew 1:18-23 (NT)
2. Born of the seed of Abraham – Genesis 17:7 (OT); Matthew 1:1 (NT)
3. Has eternal existence – Micah 5:2 (OT); John 1:1 (NT)

4. Hated without reason – Psalm 35:19 (OT); John 15:24-25 (NT)
5. Anointed by God – Psalm 45:6–7 (OT); Hebrews 1:8–9 (NT)
6. Healer, miracle worker, and Savior – Isaiah 35:4–6 (OT); John 9:1–7 (NT)
7. Accused by false witnesses – Psalm 27:12 (OT); Matthew 26:60 (NT)
8. Sold for 30 pieces of silver – Zechariah 11:12 (OT); Matthew 26:14–15 (NT)
9. Raised from the dead – Psalm 16:8–11 (OT); Luke 24:6–8 (NT)
10. Sinless and without guile – Isaiah 53:9 (OT); 1 Peter 2:22 (NT)
11. Made into an offering for sin – Isaiah 53:10–11 (OT); Acts 10:43; 13:38 (NT)
12. The "I Am" (Jehovah) – Exodus 3:13–15 (OT); John 8:24; 13:19 (NT)
13. Promised Redeemer – Isaiah 59:20 (OT); Galatians 4:4–5 (NT)
14. Son of God – Psalm 2:7 (OT); Mark 1:11; Acts 13:33 (NT)
15. Immanuel, God with us – Isaiah 7:14; 8:8-10 (OT); John 1:14; 14:8–11 (NT)

Based on solid biblical evidence, an individual can see that Jesus is just who He claimed to be; the Messiah, or Savior and Lord. Others, such as Peter, also claimed Him to be the Christ. More importantly, Jesus showed that His claims were indeed true by fulfilling messianic prophecies, thus He removed any doubt about His claims. The book of Revelation in the New Testament presents a few prophecies that are still to be fulfilled.

The Bible: The Word of God

The Bible was so uniquely written that no other religious sacred or holy book can even come close to it. An examination of the

Scriptures relates some amazing facts about the Bible (the Word of God) in terms of the way it was written and brought together. A task of this magnitude could have come about only by the inspiration of God since it is not possible for a finite human mind to come up with something this unique.

According to Webster's dictionary, the word unique is defined as "one and only; different from all others; and having no equal." Based on this definition, the Bible is unquestionably a unique book. It is unique in terms of its circulation, translation and survival through time, persecution, and criticism; its teachings through prophecy, history, and character; its influence on literature, and its influence on civilization. But most importantly, the Bible makes known the fact that Jesus Christ is one with the true living God.

The Bible is so special that it deserves a reserved place on each individual's desk top. It is the only book that was written over a 1,600-year span. Furthermore, it was written by more than forty authors under conditions lending themselves to different moods and from many different walks of life. It was also written in different places (on three continents) and in three different languages. Thus it was written using a wide variety of literary styles. Moreover, it deals with hundreds of controversial topics. Despite its diversity, the Bible relates a single unfolding love story about God's redemption of a sinful mankind by way of His Son, Jesus Christ.

How We Got the Bible

The Bible is the inerrant inspired Word of God (2 Timothy 3:16–17; 2 Peter 1:20–21). It comprises sixty-six books that were written over 1,600 years. The Old Testament was written mainly in Hebrew, but with some Aramaic, between 1,500 and 400 B.C.; the New Testament was written in Greek between A.D. 45 and 100.

The Latin Bible was the first book printed on the printing press (Gutenberg Press, 1455). Before that, the Scriptures were copied by hand. Much evidence shows that the Bible as it exists today is very close to its original form, thus its text has been preserved much better than the writings by Caesar, Plato, or Aristotle.

The Bible was first written on stone, clay, and leather around 1,500 B.C. But by A.D. 110, it was copied on papyrus and fine animal skins from calves, antelope (vellum), sheep, or goats (parchment). "Two of the oldest Vellum copies (A.D. 325–350) that exist today are the Vatican Codex and the Sinaitic Codex" (Rose Publishing, 2005).

The King James Version of the Bible (also known as the Authorized Version) is the translation that has withstood the greatest amount of criticism over the 400 plus years of its availability. This translation was undertaken by scholars who were commissioned by King James 1 of England. There were six teams that included a total of fifty-four scholars who worked on this translation for six years. The edition that is the most widely used today is the 1769 revised edition.

Skeptics frequently ask, "Can the Bible be trusted?" The answer is a resounding "Yes." I previously described details on how the Bible was written. But it is notable enough to mention again that it is no ordinary task for the Bible to have been written as it was unless God Himself inspired the writers of each book and each chapter.

It may not be an easy task to prove that every writer of the Bible was inspired by God to write every word in the Bible. But a God "who supernaturally created the entire universe could certainly put word-for-word ideas into the mind of human authors" (Muncaster, 2000). Furthermore, Jesus confirmed both Old and New Testaments as being truth.

Skeptics often ask why Christianity is better than all other religions in the world. They want to know why anyone should trust Christianity over Buddhism, Hinduism, Islam, or any other religion. There is no faith that even compares to the Christian faith. For example, Christianity is the only religion that offers salvation by grace and through faith; it is given as a gift to all who will receive Jesus as Savior and Lord. Other religions teach salvation by works. Furthermore, Christianity is the only faith whereby it is shown that God is in search of man. All other religions teach that man is constantly in search for God.

World-famous Christian evangelist Dr. Billy Graham stated, "There are many religions in the world, but only one Christianity, for only Christianity has a God who gave Himself for mankind. World religions attempt to reach up to God; Christianity is God reaching down to man" (Quoted in James R. Adair & Ted Miller, eds., *Escape from Darkness,* Wheaton: Victor, 1982, 51).

One of the differentiating aspects about Christianity is the belief that God has all the answers to life's problems. Other religions teach that man has the answer to all of life's problems. In his book *Christianity for Skeptics,* Dr. Steve Kumar states, "Christianity answers the questions of history, offers a solution to the problem of sin, removes the burden of guilt, releases from the fear of death, reverses despair into hope, and provides power to live a victorious life with God" (Kumar, 2000).

The Christian faith is the only belief that gives an account of the resurrection of Jesus Christ. The author G. B. Hardy states,

> There are but two essential requirements: 1) has anyone cheated death and proved it? and 2) is it available to me? Here is the complete record: Confucius' Tomb—Occupied; Buddha's Tomb —Occupied; Muhammad's Tomb—Occupied; and Jesus' Tomb—EMPTY. Argue as you will…There is no point in following a loser.
>
> —G. B. Hardy, Countdown, 32

None of the founders of other world religions have ever conquered their own death, and that in and of itself lends enough proof that they do not represent the truth. Conversely, Jesus Christ claimed to be truth (John 14:6) and proved it by rising from the grave. The greatest enemy or fear of human beings is death, which Jesus Christ conquered by His resurrection. This event alone makes Jesus the greatest authority on truth. Thus, only Jesus has a legitimate right to speak authoritatively on issues related to God, life, and death.

Christianity is considered to be both special and unique. Christian author Dr. Steve Kumar states that in Jesus Christ "our sins are forgiven, our guilt is removed, our fear of death is destroyed, our faith is founded on a personal God, our search for truth is satisfied, our security and identity are complete, and our lives are now based on a new hope" (Kumar, 2000).

The Bible verse that most touched my heart when I was searching for the truth as it relates to God is found in Psalms:

> I waited patiently for the Lord; and He inclined to me, and heard my cry. He also brought me up out of a horrible pit, out of the miry clay, and set my feet upon a rock, and established my steps. He has put a new song in my mouth—Praise to our God; Many will see it and fear, and will trust in the Lord"
> —Psalm 40:1–3, NKJV

Finally, the only options for consideration are that either Jesus is true and all other religions are false or other religions are true and Jesus is false. Indeed, all the other religions do not teach the same truth since many of them contradict one another. If they all cannot be true, I believe that Jesus is who He said that He was and that what He said is truth.

Each individual has to make a choice on his own, either to trust in Jesus and what He said or to reject Him and His teachings. It is my sincere prayer that each individual who reads this book will make the right decision. It is a decision that cannot be taken lightly as it will determine where an individual will spend eternity—in heaven or hell.

SECTION SEVEN

THE CONCLUSION

CHAPTER 31

MY PERSONAL TESTIMONY

IN AUGUST 1982, I came to the United States to further my education. I lived with my eldest brother and his family for about twenty-one months while I earned an associate degree.

I experienced a lot of homesickness during this time since I had never before been away from my parents and other siblings for an extended period of time. Furthermore, being away from the home of my birth presented even greater challenges and difficulties for me from an emotional standpoint since as the youngest of eight siblings I was accustomed to getting a lot of special attention. But at the same time I was glad to be getting away from such close oversight since this allowed me more time and opportunity to focus on seeking answers to questions that I had about God, peace, and happiness. It also allowed me more time to find out why I felt so lost, confused, and lonely from a spiritual standpoint. My search for spiritual truth began by reading books at the college library as well as doing research by asking individuals about their particular religious belief system.

After graduating with an associate degree in May 1984, I transferred to a four-year university that was many miles away from my eldest brother and his family. This move allowed me to have even more time to seek answers to my spiritual questions.

While on campus at this university, I met a man of God who wanted to witness to me about his beliefs in the Bible and Jesus. I asked him if he knew anything about Hinduism, but I could tell that he was not interested in what I believed. Yet he agreed to meet with me in the cafeteria one week later so that we could exchange information on our belief systems. To my surprise, though, this man of God did not show up for this meeting.

When our paths crossed at a later date, he apologized for missing this meeting but did not offer any reasons for not showing up. At a follow-up meeting, I could tell that he was uneasy reading Hindu beliefs. I interpreted his uneasiness to mean that he was narrow-minded in his thinking and I lost interest in speaking with him and others about any spiritual matters.

I had also made friends with some Muslims at that time, and we spent quite a lot of time playing chess and going to movies. But mostly we discussed and shared our religious beliefs. Furthermore, I made friends with some Buddhists, and we spent a lot of time discussing and sharing our belief systems as well.

In June of 1985 I met an individual who told me about a Christian television program (700 Club) that was hosted by Pat Robertson and which aired each evening from midnight until 1:00 am. Thus I decided to watch it in order to get information on what Christians believed instead of trying to speak with seemingly narrow-minded Christians. The first three months of viewing this program turned out to be very entertaining. But by September of that same year, I found myself getting hooked into viewing it. Yet I was somewhat confused as to how a strong Hindu Brahmin like myself was becoming so attracted to watching this program each night.

On January 12, 1986, while on a date with my girlfriend dancing in a bar, I told her that I had to leave right away in order to be back to my apartment in time to watch that Christian television program. My girlfriend was not happy and insisted that I stay. But I told her that I did not want to miss that show at any cost even though I was still a Hindu Brahmin.

I arrived at my apartment just in time to see the program. But what happened that morning changed my life forever. At the midnight I turned my television and heard Pat Robertson, host of the 700 club say,

> There is a young man who just turned the television on. This young man comes from the East. All his life he has served other gods, but deep inside he was not happy or at peace. For the last three years, he has been seeking and searching for the truth.
>
> Many Christian men have approached him to witness and share the gospel, but this young man was disappointed with their narrow-mindedness and, thus, shoved all of them off. Someone told him about this show and he started to watch it. Young man, I want you to know that God knows you and understands you and He loves you very much. The Bible says to 'seek Him while He may yet be found' (Is. 55:6) and the Bible also says, 'Behold, now is the day of salvation' (2 Cor. 6:2.) Please do not let this day go by as it may never come again.

As soon as he said all that, I began to cry like a baby. My body stated to shiver (as though I was freezing), and I lost my balance and fell to the floor but did not get hurt. I could not reason nor understand what was happening to me. At that very moment, with what little knowledge I had about Jesus or the Bible, and with a childlike faith, I accepted Jesus Christ as my personal Lord and Savior, and became a born-again Christian based on John 3:3, 7.

Although I was very happy and at peace within myself, I still had a lot of other issues concerning my family and personal life that were troubling me. For example, what could I say to my family to explain about my conversion and how would they react to it? Even though, I did not receive a lot of objection from their end, I still felt uncomfortable because of wondering what they might be thinking.

I was also experiencing some emotional and academic struggles. For example, I failed all of my courses (receiving six F's), which brought my GPA to right around 1.45. That resulted in my being placed on academic probation. My relationship with my best friend also ended at that time. Furthermore, I was deluged by doubts as to what had happened to me. These unresolved issues led me to thoughts of suicide, which culminated in my making three failed attempts. Even though I was not aware at the time, I believe that none of these attempts worked as God was watching over me and protecting me.

In my first failed attempt, I went to the train track located a few miles away from campus and contemplated lying on the track before the train passed by me. But I found out later that that particular day was the only day over the past ten years or so that the train did not make its scheduled trip. In my second failed attempt, I purchased fifty to sixty over-the-counter pills and mixed them with soup and then consumed it. But nothing happened to me.

In my third failed attempt, I went without sleep for a couple of days before driving 70 mph on a highway in the middle of the night. In doing so, I was hoping that I might fall asleep and hit a big semi truck and that would be the end of my life and problems. But even that did not work. In the past I had tried to fall asleep while driving on the highway on two separate occasions. On both of these occasions, I was the only driver other than the police officer who woke me up. Each time, I took a u-turn in the middle of my sleep and did not know it. I would start heading in one direction (west) and next thing I knew I was heading in the opposite direction (east). It had to be a miracle, meaning divine intervention.

As a last resort, I thought that I would buy some gasoline and burn myself. I remembered crying continuously from 11:00 am until about 3:00 pm, when I must have fallen asleep. In the middle of the night, I woke up and was aware of some bright light. Although I was very much awake, I was unable to open my eyes despite having tried as hard as I possibly could. I remembered thinking that I would probably have gone blind if I had been able to open my eyes. And the fact that I could not open them must have worked in my favor.

I kept saying out loud "Please go away and leave me alone because I deserve to go to hell." Then I felt as if the Lord was whispering the following words in my ears: "Fear not, I am the resurrected one. I see what is happening, and in the days and months to come I will give you an understanding of what is going on. I will use you in a mighty way that you know not. Many people will come into my kingdom because of you." These words comforted me and the voice sounded like one that had all the nine fruit of the Spirit blended into one—it was an awesome voice!

My immediate reaction was that I probably had had a dream, and I dismissed the experience, while continually doubting all that had happened to me. But the following Sunday, our church—I had started attending a Christian church soon after my conversion—invited a traveling evangelist to speak. This man of God had a prophetic word for me. Although he had never before met me and had no idea as to what I was going through, he repeated the exact same words that I heard whispered into my ears while I was seemingly dreaming. This event convinced me that the message that I had heard must have come from the Lord.

All of these events happened just three months after I became a born-again believer. Usually, people experience some kind of trauma or stress first and then get saved. But In my case, suffering continued even after I received salvation.

I now believed beyond any shadow of doubt that I had made the right decision by accepting Jesus as my personal Lord and Savior. Approximately one year later, on Easter, 1987, I shared my personal testimony on the 700 Club, which was being telecast in about seventy countries and watched by several hundred millions of people worldwide.

Although I have not always lived faithfully for the Lord with so many unconfessed and unrepented repeated sins against my wife (Victoria, a very godly woman, whom I married in August of 1992) and against other believers, God has always been faithful in extending His mercy, love, compassion, and forgiveness to me. I consider my wife to be a God-loving and God-fearing woman with much wisdom and she is a true blessing. My life can probably best be summed up as follows: "I once used God; now He is using me." It is my sincere prayer that non-believers and skeptics who read this book will keep an open mind to its spiritual content. I also hope that those individuals who are sincerely seeking the truth will find it and they can be assured of that as promised in the Bible: "…And those who seek me diligently will find me" (Proverbs 8:17, NKJV).

A Model Salvation Prayer

When an individual is ready to pray and accept Jesus as his personal Lord and Savior, I believe that God will give him the words to say in prayer and that those words will agree with their spirit. But the most important thing is that whatever people confess with their mouth and believe in their heart, they will need to make sure that they wholeheartedly mean what they pray. But here is a model salvation prayer:

Dear God,

I am a sinner and have lived a sinful life. I am not proud of the things that I have said and also not proud of my actions. I have offended not only You but also many others, which includes my family, friends, and others, such as strangers and acquaintances. I have lived a selfish (self-centered) life and cared only for myself.

I am asking you to please forgive me of my sins. I believe that Jesus died on the cross for my sins and I also believe that only through Him can my sins be forgiven. I now confess with my mouth and believe in my heart that Jesus is Lord and Savior, and I am ready to accept Jesus as my personal Lord and Savior. Please come into my heart and life and help me to live a godly life. I want to surrender my all to You and I want to live for You and also want to serve You and others. Please use me in your kingdom. I now thank You for accepting me as your child. Thank You. I ask and pray this in Jesus' precious and mighty name.

Amen.

A Final Note

This book presents the facts about the teachings and central beliefs of Christianity, Hinduism, Buddhism and Islam. I strongly suggest that readers carefully compare the evidence that each religion presents and study the content of this evidence while keeping an open mind and objectivity concerning their thoughts on each religion. All the evidence presented in this book points strongly in only one direction. It points toward Jesus Christ wherein there is truth as it relates to God. There is a famous saying from the Lord Jesus Himself that is a fitting end to this book: "And you shall know the truth, and the truth shall make you free" (John 8:32, NKJV).

I pray that you, too, will seek and find the truth as it relates to God and that you, too, will choose to accept it.

In Jesus' Love and Service,
Raj.
A Servant at Heart

BIBLIOGRAPHY

Anderson, Sir Norman. *Islam in the Modern World.* Leicester, England: Inter-Varsity Press, 1990.

Ankerberg, John, and Burroughs, Dillon. *What's the Big Deal About Other Religions?* Eugene, OR: Harvest House Publishers, 2008.

Bhalla, Prem. *Hindu Rites, Rituals, Customs, & Traditions.* New Delhi, India: Pustak Mahal, 2007.

Bickel, Bruce and Jantz, Stan. *World Religions & Cults 101: A Guide to Spiritual Beliefs.* Eugene, OR: Harvest House Publishers, 2002.

Bickel, Bruce and Jantz, Stan. *Guide to Cults, Religions, and Spiritual Beliefs.* Eugene, OR: Harvest House Publishers, 2002.

Bonaparte, Napoleon. Quoted from Grounds, Vernon C. *The Reason For Our Hope.* Chicago, IL: Moody Press, 1945.

Braswell Jr, George. *Understanding World Religions.* Nashville, TN: Broadman & Holman Publishers, 1994.

Cowan, Steve. "Apologetics: The Logical Presentation and Defense of the Christian Faith." www.ApologeticsIndex.com, 2009.

Cowper, William. "God Works in Mysterious Ways." Referring to Habakkuk-1:5.

Delgoda, Tammita. *A Traveler's History of India*. Bangalore, India: Master Mind Books, 2000.

Descartes, René. Quoted from the book *Words from the Wise*. New York, NY: Skyhorse Publishing, 2007.

Dashti, Ali. *Twenty-Three Years: A Study of the Prophetic Career of Mohammad*. London, England: Allen & Unwin, 1985.

Encyclopedia Britannica. "Basic Beliefs of Hinduism." May 19th, 2008.

Eternal Ministries. "What Do Hindus Believe?" www.EternalMinistries.com, 2009.

Etue, Kate and Baker, Tim. *Why So Many Gods?* Nashville, TN: Thomas Nelson, Inc., 2002.

Geisler, Norman and Zacharias, Ravi. *Who Made God?* Grand Rapids, MI: Zondervan, 2003.

Graham, Billy. Quoted from James R. Adair & Ted Miller, eds. *Escape from Darkness*. Wheaton, IL: Victor Books, 1982.

Grudem, Wayne. *Systematic Theology*. Downers Grove, IL: InterVarsity Press, 1994.

Halverson, Dean. *The Illustrated Guide to World Religions*. Bloomington, MN: Bethany House Publishers, 2003.

Hancock, Mary E. *Womanhood in the Making: Domestic Ritual and Public Culture in Urban South India*. Boulder, CO: Westview Press, 1999.

Harber, Frank. "How to Respond to 10 Common Objections to Christianity." w ww.ChristianityToday.com, 2007.

Harber, Frank. "Ten Objections to Christianity and How to Respond." www.ChristianityToday.com, 2000-2009.

Hardy, G.B. *Countdown*. Chicago, IL: Moody Press, 1970.

Himalayan Academy. "Nine Beliefs of Hinduism." www. HimalayanAcademy.com, 2009.

Hinnells, John R. *The Penguin Dictionary of Religions.* New York, NY: Penguin Books Ltd, 1997.

Holy Bible. King James Bible: *Jack Van Impe Prophecy Bible.* Troy, MI.

Holy Bible. New King James Version. The Open Bible: Expanded Edition. Nashville, TN: Thomas Nelson, 1982.

Holy Qur'an.

Iskcon. *Heart of Hinduism.* New York, NY: International Society for Krishna Consciousness, 2004.

Jayaram, V. "Brahma, Vishnu, and Shiva." www.HinduWebsite. com, 2000-2007.

Jayaram, V. "Saraswathi, Lakshmi, and Parvathi." www. HinduWebsite.com, 2000-2007.

Jayaram, V. "The Bhagavad-Gita Home Page." www.HinduWebsite. com, 2000-2007.

Jayaram, V. "Principles and Practice of Karma Yoga." www. HinduWebsite.com, 2000-2007.

Jayaram, V. "Jnana Yoga" and "Bhakti Yoga." www.HinduWebsite. com, 2000-2007.

Johnsen, Linda. *The Complete Idiot's Guide to Hinduism.* New York, NY: Penguin Group, 2002.

Krishnananda, Swami. http//www.swami-krishnananda.org/ brahma/brahma 01.html.

Kumar Steve. *Christianity for Skeptics.* Peabody, MA: Hendrickson Publishers, 2000.

Lewis, C. S. *Mere Christianity.* New York, NY: Macmillan, 1952.

McDermott, Gerald. *Can Evangelicals Learn from World Religions?* Downers Grove, IL: InterVarsity Press, 2000.

McDowell, Josh. *Christianity Compared with Other Religions.* Nashville, TN: Thomas Nelson, 1993.

McDowell, Josh. *Evidence for Christianity.* Nashville, TN: Thomas Nelson, 2006.

McDowell, Josh and Stewart, Don. *Answers to Tough Questions.* Wheaton, IL: Tyndale House Publishers, Inc., 1980.

Miller, William. *A Christian's Response to Islam.* Phillipsburg, NJ: Presbyterian and Reformed Publishing Company, 1976.

Mitchell, Stephen. *Bhagavad-Gita.* New York, NY: Three Rivers Press, 2000.

Muncaster, Ralph. *Can You Trust the Bible?* Eugene, OR: Harvest House Publishers, 2000.

Muncaster, Ralph. *What is the Trinity?* Eugene, OR: Harvest House Publishers, 2001.

Muncaster, Ralph. *Evidence for Jesus.* Eugene, OR: Harvest House Publishers, 2004.

Muncaster, Ralph. *Examine the Evidence: Exploring the Case for Christianity.* Eugene, OR: Harvest House Publishers, 2004.

Nehru, Jawaharlal. *The Discovery of India.* Calcutta, India: The Signet Press, 1946.

Noss, B. *Man's Religions.* New York, NY: Macmillan Publishing Company,

Oxford Desk Dictionary & Thesaurus, 2nd Edition. Oxford University Press. New York, NY: Spark Publishing, 2007.

Pollock, Robert. *The Everything World Religions Book.* Avon, MA: Adams Media, 2002.

Pratte, David E. "Buddhism & Christianity." w ww.TheGospelWay.com, 2000.

Pratte, David E. "Hinduism & Christianity." www.TheGospelWay.com, 2000.

Pratte, David E. "Islam or Christianity?" www.TheGospelWay. com, 2000.

Robertson, Pat. *Answers to 200 of Life's Most Probing Questions.* Nashville, TN: Thomas Nelson Publishers, 1984.

Rhodes, Ron. *Islam: What You Need to Know.* Eugene, OR: Harvest House Publishers, 2000.

Rhodes, Ron. *Reasoning from the Scriptures with Muslims.* Eugene, OR: Harvest House Publishers, 2002.

Rhodes, Ron. *World Religions: What You Need to Know.* Eugene, OR: Harvest House Publishers, 2007.

Rood, Rick. "Hinduism." www.ProbeMinistries.com, 2009.

Ross, Kelley. "The Caste System and the Stages of Life in Hinduism." www.friesian.com, 2009.

Russo, Steve. *They All Can't Be Right: Do All Spiritual Paths Lead to God?* Nashville, TN: Broadman and Holman Publishers, 2004.

Safa, Reza. *Inside Islam: Exposing and Reaching the World of Islam.* Lake Mary, FL: Charisma House, 1996.

Schaeffer, Francis. Taken from the book *World Religions & Cults 101* by Bruce Bickel &Stan Jantz. Eugene, OR: Harvest House Publishers, 2002.

Slick, Matthew. "Comparison Grid between Christianity and Islamic Doctrine." ww.carm.org, 1995-2008.

Slick, Matthew. "Objections and Answers." www.carm.org, 1995-2008.

Somany, Ganga. *Hinduism: An Illustrative Introduction.* New Delhi, India: Bookwise Private Limited, 2003.

Sproul, R.C. *Reason to Believe.* Grand Rapids, MI: Zondervan, 1978.

Sproul, R.C. *Now, That's a Good Question.* Wheaton, IL: Tyndale House Publishers, 1996.

Toropov, Brandon and Father Buckles. *The Complete Idiot's Guide to World Religions.* New York, NY: Penguin Group, 2004.

Water, Mark. *The Bible Made Plain and Simple.* Peabody, MA: Hendrickson Publishers Inc., 1999.

Water, Mark. *Encyclopedia of World Religions, Cults, and the Occult.* Chattanooga, TN: AMG Publishers, 2006.

Webster's Dictionary, Fourth Edition. New York, NY: Ballantine Books, 2001.

Woods, Len. *Handbook of World Religions.* Uhrichsville, OH: Barbour Publishing Inc., 2008.

Wright, Rusty. "7 Questions Skeptics Ask." www.Probe.Org, , 2007.

www.About-Jesus.org

www.carm.com

www.ChristianityToday.com

www.ContenderMinistsries.com

www.EternalMinistries.com

www.Gita.com

www.imahal.com

www.Probe.org

www.RosePublishing.com

www.TheGospelWay.com

www.100Prophecies.org

Yancey, Philip. *Church: Why Bother?: My Personal Pilgrimage.* Grand Rapids, MI: Zondervan, 2001.

Zacharias, Ravi. *Jesus Among Other Gods: The Absolute Claims of the Christian Message.* Nashville, TN: Word Publishing, 2000.

Zukeran, Patrick. www.ProbeMinistries.com, 2009.

REFERENCE TO THE HINDU SCRIPTURES

Bhagavad-Gita

2:13
2:22
2:47
2:64-65
2:71
3:9
4:8
6:1
6:45
9:34
12:8-9
18:6

The Vedas

Rig Veda

Rig-Veda-I.91.7.
Rig-Veda-I.116.19.
Rig-Veda-II.12.2.
Rig-Veda-III.31.1-2.
Rig-Veda-VI.55.4 (Apte-11).
Rig-Veda-X.3.3. (Apte-11).
Rig-Veda-X.121.1.
Riv-Veda-X.173.4.

Satapatha Brahmana-XIII.9. - (Apte-63)

Yajur-Veda

Yajur-Veda-4.30.
Yajur-Veda-5.16.
Yajur-Veda-13.56-57.
Yajur-Veda-14.5.

REFERENCE TO THE
HOLY BIBLE

The Old Testament

Genesis 1:1–2

Genesis 1:26, 28

Genesis 7:1–7

Genesis 8:4

Genesis 11:27

Genesis 12:1

Genesis-17:7

Genesis-20:6

Exodus 2:5

Exodus 3:13–15

Exodus 20:2–5

Exodus-31:3

Exodus 34:27

Numbers 24:2–3

Deuteronomy 6:4

Deuteronomy 18:10–14

1 Samuel 15:29

2 Samuel 23:2

1 Chronicles 28:19

Job 5:7

Job 11:7–9

Job 38:4–5

Psalm 2:7

Psalm 8:3–6

Psalm 16:8–11

Psalm 19:1–2, 7

Psalm 27:12

Psalm 35:19

Psalm 40:1–3

Psalm 45:3–7

Psalm 46:1

Psalm 50:15

Psalm 51:4

Psalm 90:2

P salm139:1–4

Psalm 139:7–3

Proverbs 5:21

Proverbs 8:17

Proverbs 23:7

Ecclesiastes 7:20

Ecclesiastes 12:7, 13
Isaiah 1:18, 20
Isaiah 6:3
Isaiah 7:14
Isaiah 8:8–10
Isaiah 9:6–7
Isaiah 35:4–6
Isaiah 38:1–6
Isaiah 43:10
Isaiah 53:9–11
Isaiah 55:6, 8
Isaiah 59:2, 20

Isaiah 64:6
Jeremiah 36:1–2
Ezekiel 18:23
Ezekiel 33:11
Daniel 8:1
Hosea 4:6
Jonah 3:1–10
Micah 5:2
Micah 6:8
Habakkuk 1:13
Zechariah 11:12
Malachi 3:6

The New Testament

Matthew 1:1
Matthew 1:18–23
Matthew 2:1
Matthew 3:15–17
Matthew 4:3
Matthew 5:44
Matthew 7:14
Matthew 7:22–23
Matthew 8:23–27
Matthew 9:13
Matthew 10:30
Matthew 12:7
Matthew 16:16–17
Matthew 19:26
Matthew 20:16, 28
Matthew 22:23–33
Matthew 22:37–40
Matthew 24:4, 37
Matthew 25:31–46
Matthew 26:14–15
Matthew 26:60
Matthew 27:23–56

Matthew 28:1–10, 19
Mark 1:1, 11
Mark 6:48–51
Luke 1:5
Luke 1:13, 20, 24, 35
Luke 1:57–64
Luke 2:6–7, 26
Luke 5:4–11, 20
Luke 6:14–16
Luke 12:48
Luke 16:19–26
Luke 19:10, 34
Luke 20:36
Luke 23:34
Luke 24:6–8, 13, 27
Luke 24:32, 34
John 1:1, 14, 25
John 1:29, 34
John 2:19–21
John 3:3, 7
John 3:16, 17
John 4:24

John 5:39

John 6:19, 29, 35

John 6:40, 48, 51

John 8:12, 24, 32

John 8:33, 46, 58

John 9:17

John 10:11, 14, 30

John 10:35–36

John 11:24

John11:43–44

John 13:19

John 14:6

John 14:8–11

John 14:16–17, 26

John 15:24–26

John 16:7

John 17:17

John 17:20–21

John 19:17–18

John 20:28

John 21:1–11

Acts 1:8

Acts 2:36

Acts 4:12

Acts 10:3

Acts 10:25–26

Acts 10:34–35, 43

Acts 13:33, 38

Acts 14:15

Acts 17:29

Acts 17:29

Acts 24:15

Romans 1:19–20

Romans 1:28–32

Romans 3:12, 23

Romans 5:6, 8

Romans 6:23

Romans 8:1–4, 13

Romans 8:17–18, 28

Romans 9:32

Romans 10:9, 12

Romans 10:13–17

Romans 13:11

Romans 14:8–10, 23

1 Corinthians 1:22

1 Corinthians 2:9

1 Corinthians 2:14–16

1 Corinthians 6:19

1 Corinthians 9:22

1 Corinthians 10:11

1 Corinthians 12:4–6

1 Corinthians 12:8–10

1 Corinthians 12:12–14

1 Corinthians 13:13

1 Corinthians 15:14, 17

1 Corinthians 15:50–58

2 Corinthians 5:8

2 Corinthians 5:17–18

2 Corinthians 6:2, 7

2 Corinthians 12:10–12

Galatians 2:21

Galatians 4:4–5

Galatians 5:22–23

Galatians 6:7

Ephesians 2:1, 3

Ephesians 2:8–10

Ephesians 4:5–6, 30

Ephesians 5:25–28

Philippians 1:21–24

Philippians 2:3–4

Philippians 2:9–11

Philippians 4:8

Colossians 2:9
1 Thessalonians 4:16–18
1 Timothy 1:17
1 Timothy 2:5
2 Timothy 1:1
2 Timothy 2:15
2 Timothy 3:15–17
Titus 2:13–14
Titus 3:3–7
Hebrews 1:1–3
Hebrews 1:8–9
Hebrews 2:6–9
Hebrews 4:12
Hebrews 9:26–28
Hebrews 13:8

James 1:18
James 2:26
James 4:7, 17
1 Peter 2:11, 22, 24
1 Peter 3:15, 20
2 Peter 1:19–21
1 John 3:4
1 John 4:1, 8
1 John 5:11
Revelation 1:8
Revelation 15:4
Revelation 19:6, 13, 16
Revelation 20:11–15
Revelation 21:6
Revelation 22:13, 16

REFERENCE TO THE HOLY QUR'AN

Sura-2:29	Sura-2:97	Sura-2:106	Sura-2:118-119
Sura-2:142	Sura-2:180	Sura-2:190	Sura-2:219
Sura-2:256	Sura-3:7	Sura-3:20	Sura-3:32
Sura-3:41	Sura-3:42	Sura-3:45	Sura-3:46
Sura-3:57	Sura-3:59	Sura-3:157	Sura-3:181-184
Sura-3:191	Sura-4:3	Sura-4:7	Sura-4:11
Sura-4:15	Sura-4:16	Sura-4:34	Sura-4:48
Sura-4:78	Sura-4:79	Sura-4:116	Sura-4:117-120
Sura-4:136	Sura-4:153	Sura-4:157	Sura-5:47-52
Sura-5:68	Sura-5:73-75	Sura-5:90	Sura-5:116
Sura-6:8-9	Sura-6:12	Sura-6:34	Sura-6:37
Sura-6:61	Sura-6:74	Sura-6:85	Sura-6:101
Sura-6:115	Sura-6:142	Sura-7:31	Sura-7:54
Sura-8:38-39	Sura-9:3	Sura-9:5	Sura-9:23
Sura-9:29	Sura-10:3	Sura-10:95	Sura-10:100
Sura-11:7	Sura-11:42	Sura-11:44	Sura-11:114
Sura-12:2	Sura-12:111	Sura-13:37	Sura-15:29

Sura-16:93	Sura-16:101	Sura-16:102	Sura-16:103
Sura-16:128	Sura-17:15	Sura-17:98-99	Sura-18:31
Sura-18:89-98	Sura-19:7	Sura-19:10	Sura-19:17-21
Sura-19:19	Sura-19:23	Sura-19:88-92	Sura-20:55
Sura-21:7	Sura-22:23	Sura-22:47	Sura-23:12
Sura-23:117	Sura-24:2	Sura-25:33	Sura-25:59
Sura-25:68-71	Sura-26:171	Sura-28:8-9	Sura-29:23
Sura-29:46	Sura-29:48-51	Sura-29:58	Sura-30:9
Sura-31:15	Sura-31:28	Sura-32:5	Sura-32:9
Sura-32:11	Sura-33:37	Sura-33:50-51	Sura-34:7
Sura-35:1	Sura-35:8	Sura-35:15	Sura-35:18
Sura-39:4	Sura-39:42	Sura-41:9-12	Sura-41:16
Sura-41:30	Sura-41:41	Sura-41:44	Sura-42:11
Sura-44:54	Sura-45:14	Sura-47:15	Sura-47:27
Sura-49:27-30	Sura-50:16	Sura-51:56	Sura-51:57
Sura-54:19	Sura-56:7	Sura-57:21	Sura-61:6
Sura-67:2	Sura-69:6-7	Sura-70:4	Sura-74:31
Sura-75:3-4	Sura-75:12	Sura-75:22-23	Sura-78:32
Sura-83:25	Sura-89:27-30	Sura-90:18-19	Sura-98:6
Sura-99:6-8	Sura-112:3		

ABOUT THE AUTHOR

Raj Vemuri was born into a large, well-educated family in India that belongs to the Hindu Brahmin caste. He came to the United States in the fall of 1982 to pursue higher education. At the same time, he was also seeking and searching for the truth as it related to God. On January 13, 1986 (at the midnight hour), he accepted Jesus Christ as his personal Lord and Savior. He has been serving the Lord ever since. His heart's desire is to fulfill God's perfect plan for his life. Raj lives in Florida with his wife, Victoria, and daughter Danielle.

EDUCATION

PhD in Clinical Christian Counseling, Cornerstone University, Lake Charles, LA

ThD in Restorative Justice, Therpon University, U.S. Virgin Islands

EdD in Counseling Psychology, Argosy University, Sarasota, FL

MA in Counseling, Liberty University, Lynchburg, VA

BBA in Marketing, Eastern Michigan University, Ypsilanti, MI

CERTIFICATIONS

Temperament Counselor, NCCA, Sarasota, FL

Marriage & Family Therapist, NCCA, Sarasota, FL

Substance Abuse & Addiction Therapist, NCCA, Sarasota, FL

Professional Pastoral Therapist, NAFC, Beaumont, TX

Belief Therapist, Therapon Institute, Marrero, LA

Re-Entry Crisis Counselor, Therapon Institute, Marrero, LA

LICENSES

Clinical Pastoral Counselor, NCCA, Sarasota, FL

Clinical Christian Counselor, NCCA, Sarasota, FL

Belief Therapist, Therapon Institute, Marrero, LA

ORDINATION

Minister of Pastoral Counseling, NCCC, Sarasota, FL

Chaplain, Chaplain Fellowship Ministries, Temple, TX

TEACHING EXPERIENCE

Adjunct Instructor of Psychology, Tallahassee Community College, Tallahassee, FL

Adjunct Instructor of Psychology, Caldwell College, Caldwell, NJ

Adjunct Instructor of Psychology, Brookdale Community College, Lincroft, NJ

Adjunct Instructor of Psychology, Essex Community College, Newark, NJ

Adjunct Instructor of Psychology, Middlesex County College, Edison, NJ

Adjunct Instructor of Psychology, Fairleigh Dickinson University, Atlantic City, NJ

SPEAKING ENGAGEMENTS

Assembly of God: Full-Gospel Businessmen's Association, Kalamazoo, MI

Cody Pentecostal Holiness Church, Monticello, FL

Tallavana Community Church, Havana, FL

New Light Church, Woodville, FL

Center For Biblical Studies, Tallahassee, FL

TV APPEARANCE

700 Club – Shared Personal Testimony – Aired on Easter Sunday, 1987

COUNSELING EXPERIENCE

Cody Pentecostal Holiness Church, Monticello, FL

Faith Horizon Ministry, Thomasville, GA

Tallavana Community Church, Havana, FL

BOARD MEMBER

Board Member – Morning Star Counseling Center, Kalamazoo, MI

Abbreviations Explained

NCCA: National Christian Counselors Association

NAFC: National Association of Faith-Based Counselors

NCCC: National Conservative Christian Church

PW

CPSIA information can be obtained at www.ICGtesting.com
Printed in the USA
LVOW051005070712

289015LV00002B/265/P